4.00
E5

JOURNALISM
TOMORROW

JOURNALISM
TOMORROW

Edited by Wesley C. Clark

Dean, School of Journalism

Syracuse University

SYRACUSE UNIVERSITY PRESS

Library of Congress Catalog Card Number: 58-13727

© 1958, SYRACUSE UNIVERSITY PRESS

MANUFACTURED IN THE UNITED STATES OF AMERICA BY
BOOK CRAFTSMEN ASSOCIATES, INC., NEW YORK

Foreword

IT IS NEARLY ONE HUNDRED years since General Robert E. Lee first attempted to establish a college program of training in journalism at Washington College, now Washington and Lee University. It is more than fifty years since Nicholas Murray Butler, president of Columbia University, and Charles W. Eliot, President of Harvard University, laid the groundwork for the great debate which still continues about the nature and function of journalism education. It is just fifty years ago that the first school of journalism was started at the University of Missouri.

Next year will mark the twenty-fifth anniversary of the founding of the School of Journalism at Syracuse University, although a limited amount of journalism instruction has been offered since 1919. Yet twenty-five years before—in 1894—Chancellor James Roscoe Day, prompted possibly by the consideration which the subject was receiving in the New York City newspapers and elsewhere, had given serious thought to the establishment of a School of Journalism at Syracuse University.

This book, written by members of the faculty of the Syracuse University School of Journalism, is concerned with the road ahead in journalism. But it also provides an occasion for looking back down the road which journalism education has travelled since General Lee first proposed a system of scholarships for young men "proposing to make journalism their profession."

Originally the area of debate about journalism education encompassed the question of whether it was possible to educate for journalism. The arguments which Horace Greeley and E. L. Godkin presented against journalism education are in essence the arguments against any kind of professional education; law, medicine, nursing, library science, and all the others. The logic of experience, if not the logic of rhetoric, has proved them wrong, and the area of debate soon moved to the question: What kind of journalism education?

President Butler contended that journalism training should concern itself only with writing and editing. President Eliot wanted not only editorial training, but also training in the whole area of journalism, from news writing to advertising and management. Unlike President Butler he had no fear of "practical studies."

Notable about the proposal which President Eliot made to Pulitzer in respect to journalism education is the way that it foreshadows the scope of the Harvard Graduate School of Business Administration. With singular clarity, considering the confusion engendered by the debate about journalism education, President Eliot saw that the problem of education could not be attacked piecemeal; that the editorial side of any publication could not be separated from the business side; that education of whatever nature could not be compartmentalized, and that education for journalism was no more vocational training than education in chemistry was vocational training for the man who hoped to become a chemist. For President Eliot it was not a question as to the appropriateness of practical studies, but how these studies are taught, how they are related to other disciplines and what educational ends they serve. The danger of any study whether practical or not is a shortsighted specialism in which we forget all the larger purposes of education.

Although President Eliot lost the debate with President Butler and the Pulitzer fortune went to Columbia, it is his view which has come to prevail in journalism education. To be sure there was something of the trade school in the first courses that were offered and not every school of journalism reflected President Eliot's understanding of what education is for. But on the credit side, the case method of instruction which has long been used in medicine and law and which has lately been adopted by schools of business and other professional schools, was from the outset an integral part of the teaching of journalism.

As might have been expected, journalism education ran into bitter opposition, principally from those who now find it most helpful—the editors and publishers. Opposition diminished, however, as journalism graduates proved their worth. Today journalism has won its place as a profession, and more and more the newspapers, the magazines, and the radio and television stations look to the schools of journalism for their trained personnel. New areas of journalism education have opened up— in public relations and in religious journalism, where the Syracuse University School of Journalism has pioneered. Radio and television, which were unheard-of when General Lee first proposed journalism instruction, turned from the beginning to schools of journalism for aid in staffing, and the schools have acquired an influence and status quite different from that enjoyed a generation ago in the newspaper world.

The work of the American Council on Education for Journalism is evidence of the growing closeness of the relationship between schools and the various facets of the journalism and mass communications professions. This body, which sponsors accreditation in the field of journalism, now represents every major field in mass communications. Its expenses are borne to a large degree by industry, which has come to discover that it has a vital stake in the training of young men and young women for the field of mass communications.

The professional is turning more and more to universities for research and advice. The Communications Research Center of the School of Journalism at Syracuse is evidence of this. In four years it has been called upon by nearly 100 organizations in the field of mass communications for aid and advice about research problems. The man with an earned doctorate in communications areas is now an important figure in modern journalism and related fields, especially advertising, marketing, research, merchandising, and sales.

As the schools of journalism increase in strength and usefulness there is a perceptible change in the breadth and depth of their courses of study. It is interesting to note that the strengthening of professional education has in the long run never been at the expense of liberal education. To the contrary, the spirit of the professional school, whether it be law, medicine, business, public administration or journalism, has in each case been infused more and more by the spirit of liberal education. In the early stages specific training seems all-important. As professions come of age the larger issues of education, public service and social responsibility assume greater importance. A good engineering college today is more and more a center of engineering science. Schools of journalism are still in transition but the shape of the future is clear. They too are primarily concerned with ideas and the highest possible development of intelligence, personality and character.

The role of a university is not that of a trade school or a technical institute. It is not concerned with training the fixed person for fixed duties. While we sharpen old skills and learn new ones, our deeper concern is for the viability of mind which can be effective in the novel and unpredictable situations of the future. Specialized functions will be performed with increasing effectiveness, but unless a generalized vision gives direction to these intensified skills they may be more of a danger than a help. "Where there is no vision the people perish."

A university makes no pretense of giving industry or the professions a finished product. In the case of journalism it ought to know what the leaders of our mass media say they want for today's needs, but its central and continuing interest is the broad foundation for the long-term needs of the future—the tomorrows not yet in sight. Thus there is a world of difference between a university classroom and on-the-job training. And the better the university the greater is the difference. It is not the business of a university to limit its vision to immediate goals.

Because education is a many-splendored thing at which we shall be working as long as we live, the university approaches all vocational and professional training in the spirit if not the subject matter of the liberal arts. The purpose is broadly the same. Using different disciplines we still desire to produce inquiring minds, minds independent, resourceful and creative, minds not frightened by new problems, minds trained in accuracy of observation and skilled in analysis and evaluation. We also desire to produce men who are morally and socially responsible. The measure of the maturity of a school of journalism is the degree of dedication it has to the spirit of learning and the art of critical and responsible thought.

WILLIAM PEARSON TOLLEY

Chancellor, Syracuse University

Introduction

THE NEED FOR A BOOK on the future of journalism has long been manifest. There have been a number of what might be called off-the-cuff predictions by the practitioners in the many fields of journalism, but for more than twenty years there has hardly been any serious evaluation of its future in the United States. Yet, during these years we have seen many predictions about the future of the nation as well as of mankind, ranging from its obliteration under the impact of the atomic age to its rescue by a revival of religion.

Some of the predictions made about various aspects of human endeavor in the early part of the twentieth century have come to pass. In the United States we now have a chicken in every pot and two cars in nearly every garage. We have two or three radios and at least one television set in every home. The 60,000,000 jobs that Henry Wallace in 1940 said were necessary for our economy, if it were to survive by 1960, were available by 1950—ten years ahead of the time set by Mr. Wallace.

In the face of these predictions, some of which have obviously gone astray, it might be thought that those who dared to predict the future of American journalism would place their reputations for good sense in jeopardy. There is always this possibility; there is also the possibility that an attempt to look into the future will raise the sights of men everywhere. It was with this in mind that the faculty of the School of Journalism at Syracuse University took the calculated risk of writing this book.

The idea for the volume came from Professor Roland E. Wolseley, chairman of the Magazine Department, and originator of the unique program of religious journalism inaugurated at Syracuse in 1949. He is the author or co-author of a dozen volumes, among them a book on the magazine field, two volumes based on his experiences as a Fulbright lecturer in India, and *Exploring Journalism*, a textbook used by scores of journalism schools throughout the country.

Professor Robert D. Murphy was a newspaperman before he became a teacher. For five years he has been chairman of the Newspaper Department, and at the same time has served as executive secretary of the New York State Society of Newspaper Editors.

[ix]

Professor Howard W. Palmer, whose chief post is Manager, New York Press Association, has worked for daily papers and edited a prize-winning weekly. He has collaborated with Gene Gilmore, an instructor who comes with extensive experience on smaller newspapers.

Professor Eugene S. Foster is chairman of the Radio-Television Department of Syracuse University. He has been consultant to the Federal Government on the Point Four Program, and has made several trips to the Middle East in the interests of the program.

Professor Philip Ward Burton, chairman of the Advertising Department, is the author of several hundred published articles, and most of his five books on advertising are being used by schools of journalism and business administration throughout the nation. He is a practitioner as well as a teacher, having from time to time served in industry, both as a consultant and as a creative copy chief.

Professor Robert W. Root has been an editorial writer for the Des Moines *Register* and *Tribune*, a free-lance writer and correspondent for the *Christian Science Monitor,* and since 1955 head of the Religious Journalism program at Syracuse. He is the author of two books, one of which, *Progress Against Prejudice,* has received notable acclaim. He was executive editor of Worldover Press, an international news syndicate, and has written for Religious News Service.

Frederic E. Demarest, a junior member of the faculty, has drawn upon his experience as a magazine photographer in teaching photojournalism.

Professor William P. Ehling heads the University News Bureau and also teaches public relations. He has had several years' experience on newspapers; one of his major interests in his educational work is research in mass communications.

Tribute should also be paid to Professor Laurance B. Siegfried, chairman of the Graphic Arts Department, and to Miss Evelyn Smith, who for many years has directed the Journalism Library at Syracuse. Miss Smith prepared the Bibliography and helped in many ways. Professor Siegfried contributed his advice and talent to the designing of the book.

WESLEY C. CLARK

Dean, School of Journalism

Syracuse University

Contents

JOURNALISM
TOMORROW

The Future of Mass Communications

WESLEY C. CLARK

ANY ATTEMPT TO FORECAST the future of journalism, or of the presumably broader subject, mass communications, is a perilous enterprise. The perils are not only inherent in the structure and nature of mass communications: they are to be found in the whole sea of life of which mass communications are so integral a part. And, perhaps the greatest peril to a reasonably accurate forecast of the future lies in the nature of the author himself. But this is a hazard which can hardly be avoided.

When mass communications are discussed either formally or informally there is a general tendency to assume that the discussants know in general the limits of the problem under discussion. Frequently this assumption is in error; hence, so that there may be no confusion about the scope of the subject, some limits are set forth. In the very broadest sense, almost all of the educational system might be included in the field of mass communications, but the inclusion of education, at least that part of education concerned with formal schooling, would do violence to the generally accepted concept of mass communications. Again the telephone is used in mass communications: it is one of the tools thereof. But not even the fact that millions of people use the telephone every day makes this instrument any more than a tool of mass communications. There is, however, little value in exhausting the list of those things which are not mass communications. A more sensible approach is to describe the broad outlines of what social scientists have come to know as mass communications.

The newspaper, the magazine, the book, radio, television, and the documentary movie are the principal instruments of mass communications. Included are not just the great newspapers in metropolitan areas, but all newspapers, even the smallest weeklies with but two or three hundred subscribers. Magazines of general circulation such as *Life, The Saturday Evening Post,* and *Harper's* are only the surface cream of a great host of magazines catering to the interests and needs of thousands of groups, ranging from the religious to the ridiculous, from aircraft owners to zinnia lovers. Radio and television are far more encompassing and their impact more widespread than the impact of the large networks alone.

[1]

In all of these media, there have been tremendous changes during the first half of the twentieth century, but even so, these media are functions of the society in which they operate and are shaped and molded by that society. In turn society itself is bent by developments within the media.

The interaction of society and the media of mass communications which service it already suggest a part of the future of mass communications. More light may be thrown upon this future by a close examination of one of the great problems which today besets society and the media of mass communications—the dispute over the right to know.

Increasingly our airwaves and our periodicals are filled with disputes about the right to know being abridged or destroyed. The disputants range from the President of the United States to the editor of a weekly paper with no more than two or three hundred subscribers, from the man shopping for a car to a corporation seeking new oil leases. State and national press associations have established committees to study the problem. The American Newspaper Publishers Association has fostered the publication of a book, titled *The People's Right to Know,* and written by an eminent legal authority.

Government, on all levels and in all branches, devotes more and more attention to the right to know. The House of Representatives under the leadership of Congressman John Moss of California has a subcommittee concerned with defending the right to know against encroachments by the executive branch of the federal government. Some thirty states have laws spelling out the right to know. Others have right to know clauses embedded in their constitutions. Despite these bulwarks, state legislatures, municipal councils, school boards, county boards, in fact almost every state and local legislative body has been accused of impairing the right to know in the last few years. The outcry against state administrative agencies is no less. The judiciary, federal and state, long considered fortresses guarding the rights of the people, also stand accused of nibbling away at the right to know.

What are the causes of this great debate over the right to know? Is it caused by newspapers and other media seeking to protect their profits? By politicians greedy for power? By do-gooders hoping to alleviate the ills of mankind? By bureaucrats seeking the ease of anonymity? By lawyers protecting their clients? By judges guarding their dignity? Or by the other groups too numerous to mention and perhaps too difficult to identify?

The responsibility cannot be allocated precisely among all of those engaged in the battle. It should, in fact, be assessed against none of them. They are not puppets, but they are being moved by forces which are irresistible and probably irreversible.

As these forces continue to gather momentum and power, new outbreaks in the dispute may be expected. Some of these will be easy to identify. Others, unless care is taken to defend the right to know, will be written off as part of the normal debate to be found in the intellectual life of any nation.

But what is the debate about? What is the right to know? In its simplest terms, it is the right to know those things which are necessary for survival and for the pursuit of happiness.

Nobody is arguing that man does not have the right to know those things which are necessary to his survival and for the pursuit of happiness. The argument centers about what is necessary. In essence and in this country, it might be described as a debate between those who argue that man needs to know the generalities, and those who argue that man needs to know the specifics as well. It is enough, says one side, for a man to know that less than 1 per cent of all juveniles are delinquent. Not so, says the other side; man must also know who comprise the less than 1 per cent and what did they steal and what did they do with the loot and from whom did they take it.

It includes much more than the right of the people to know about the qualifications and the records of the men or women that they are asked to vote for or against, or the right to know what are the laws and whether they are enforced equitably. The right to know includes the right to know whether the schools a man sends his children to are good or bad, whether the companions his son runs around with are hoodlums, whether the young man his daughter is crazy about is to be trusted, whether his neighbors are honest or whether they be thieves or murderers, whether the medicine he buys is safe, whether the prices he pays are equitable or whether his neighbors get better prices at the same places, whether the taxes he pays are the same as the taxes paid by other people in his circumstances; whether the doctor he goes to is well trained, whether his car is safe to drive, whether the police are honest and the judges incorruptible.

In spite of the present clamor, the plain fact is that erosion of the people's right to know has been going on for years. It was, in fact, being eaten away when President Wilson demanded "open covenants, openly arrived at," and when the battle for the right to know seemingly had been won, or nearly so.

The forces which are eroding the people's right to know are the forces which are changing this nation from a rural to an urban civilization. Primarily, these are population growth and increasing mobility, and their consequences—a vast increase in the public interest resulting in an explosive expansion in government.

Population growth needs no explanation. The figures—100 million in 1925 and 160 million in 1955 speak for themselves. The number of automobiles today as compared with 1925 documents the increase in mobility. Figures on airplanes, and other forms of mobility only provide padding.

The growth of the public interest needs explanation. The public interest may be contrasted with the private interest. Thus the sanitary arrangements of a rancher on his 10,000 acres are of little interest to the public, but the sanitary arrangements of a man who lives on a 30-foot lot in a crowded suburb are of interest, intense public interest, for he may, unless he conforms to a sanitary code, infect a whole neighborhood. In short the public interest concerns those acts which are of interest to large parts of the public and which in the interests of society must be regulated or controlled.

The enormous increase in the public interest may be measured in many ways. It can be measured in terms of the gross number of laws in force today as compared with 40 or 50 years ago. It can be measured in terms of the number of police, or rather policing officers, for the term police carries the connotation of a uniformed officer whereas in reality this nation has more police officers operating under other titles and uniforms than it has traditional uniformed police. Health and sanitation inspectors, factory inspectors, wage and hour administrators, sewer inspectors, social security investigators, soil conservation employees are all in a very real sense police officers. In fact, almost every area of government exercises some police power and exercises it through police officers whether they go under that title or some more acceptable euphemism.

Again the growth of the public interest can be measured in terms of functions operated by the federal government. In the last half century we have witnessed the extension of federal control into agriculture, into the commodity and security markets, the regulation of wages and hours, the impost of estate and income taxes, and a whole host of other areas.

The growth of the public interest can be measured in terms of the number of people affected by laws. Thus, until this century the federal government, except through the post office, touched upon the lives of comparatively few people. Now it touches upon the lives of nearly all of us again and again, through income taxes, social security, and unemployment compensation.

But, however the rate of the public interest is measured, it is apparent that it has grown enormously, much faster than the rate of population.

If we examine the impact of these great changes in American society upon the right to know, two paradoxes stand out. These changes have increased the people's knowledge, but increased far more the amount of knowledge which they need. Again these factors have made the securing of knowledge easier; and yet at the same time made it harder.

The population growth has squeezed more people into smaller areas, so that a man today has a much greater opportunity to increase his knowledge of people than he used to have. But each person he adds to his orbit increases his need for knowledge. For each person in his orbit, a man needs to know many things if he is to live with him in security and safety. It is easy to know what political clubs or beliefs are present among a small circle of acquaintances, but as a man enlarges his circle the problem becomes increasingly more difficult, but the danger of knowing the wrong individual remains as great, or rather the evil results from knowing the wrong individual remain just as great.

Man has in mid-twentieth century conquered space, but not time. The mobility which is an integral part of our modern heritage enables us to range farther and wider. It enables us to do it more quickly, but not quickly enough.

Man has only twenty-four hours a day in which to learn all of the things he needed to know a thousand years ago when he knew daily an area of fifty miles and but a thousand people. Now he daily covers an area of a thousand square miles and living therein are a million people. Theoretically he should know each of them in order to be secure in his day-to-day life. Today so many impressions crowd in upon him that he sees life not as through a glass darkly, not even as a reflection of shadows in some Grecian cave, but as a blurred succession of images, like a movie film run too fast through the projector.

Mobility in much the same way makes it easier to know far places and far people, and some not so far. The fact that we can send our children to a museum or a library four or five miles away increases their knowledge and perhaps ours, but it increases our need for knowledge, for we must know what kinds of streets they must travel, what kinds of people live in those areas, what are the best times to travel, what places might be attractive and dangerous to young people.

The growth of public interest and the consequent growth of government has created enormous communication problems for the ordinary citizen. In many cases it has been difficult if not impossible for him to determine by himself what the laws are which affect him. Thus the home builder, for instance, must rely not upon his own knowledge but upon second-hand knowledge to ascertain what the building code is and what parts of it affect him.

But even more important, he, being subject to so many laws, has little opportunity to discover whether his neighbors and the other residents of the community are being treated equally by the law and in the public interest. He has little or no first-hand knowledge to guide him: he must rely upon intermediaries to supply him with this knowledge.

The intermediaries to which the citizen turns are the media of mass

[5]

communications—the newspapers, television, radio, magazines, motion picture newsreels, news services, syndicates, and books.

But the factors of growth, mobility, and public interest influence the press no less than they do the individual.

Population growth increases the number of people who subscribe to the newspaper, but it increases the number of news possibilities not in direct proportion to the population increase, but in geometrical progression, or nearly so, because the chances for interaction are so much greater. To use a very simple illustration: if two men play golf, there are three possible outcomes. A may defeat B, or vice versa, or they may tie. But if three men play, the number of outcomes increases enormously: A may beat B and B may beat C; or A may beat C and C defeat B; or A and B may tie and both beat C; or A and C may tie and both defeat B.

If to population growth is added the factor of mobility, the possibility of additional news stories increases again. For, if instead of a stable, isolated community, five or ten thousand people move in and out of it each day, it is obvious that the number of news possibilities is increased tremendously.

But mobility not only affects the media of communications by permitting more people to come within their orbits; it permits them to enlarge their orbits. Not only can the media transport news farther and quicker, but the mobility of communication permits the gathering of news from far places, sometimes more quickly than from the nearby communities.

The speed and mobility of knowledge, undreamed of 200 years ago, makes it possible for the media to publish news from far away more cheaply and more quickly than it is possible for it to gather and publish news about the community in which it lives. With the development of the teletypesetter by the Associated Press and the United Press, it is less expensive for a newspaper to print news about India than about its own community. This is so on two counts. The cost to a newspaper is less, for although it is expensive to gather the news about India the cost is shared by many papers, hence is less for each paper. Second, it costs less to produce the news in type.

The result of this is that when a paper or any other medium is squeezed for space or for money, it is tempted to overlook those news items which are of vital local import and to concentrate upon those things which are important but distant.

It is even cheaper for the media to buy opinion than it is to employ a man to express its opinion. An example in point is the syndicated columnist. Even the most expensive of these columnists is far less expensive to a single paper than the cost of maintaining on the staff of the paper itself a writer of comparable ability, or even of the cost of maintaining a reporter under the pay scales which obtain in most sections of the country. Yet the mobility of transport permits these syndicated columns to reach a paper almost as quickly as one of its own men can write a column.

To the problems caused by population growth and mobility, the growth of government and the public interest has added a tremendous overload on our already overloaded mass communications system.

Thus an income tax law, an agricultural subsidy law, or an unemployment compensation law each adds millions of potential news possibilities, for wherever the citizen and the law meet there is a possibility of public interest or news developing. In addition, each of these laws is administered not only from Washington, but by states, by regions, by cities, and by counties. Thus what might be called the regular fountains of news, or what Lippmann called places of record, are increased a hundredfold and the media are flooded, drowned almost, in the torrent of news.

If the media were to cover these areas meaningfully, they would have to assign reporters to cover the headquarters of these agencies in their area. And again they would have to find space or time to publish the news about these activities.

The problem of helping the citizen know what he needs to know in addition to what he can know by himself is therefore an enormous one for the media of mass communication. Yet none of them is indefinitely expandable. The limits are sometimes economic, but to a large extent they are imposed by the citizen himself, and they are not necessarily economic.

Many newspapers, for instance, are covering tremendously larger populations and areas which have expanded astronomically in terms of the public interest with little more, and in fact sometimes less, manpower than they used two or three generations ago. Discounting the factor of public interest, it would seem reasonable for a paper which is serving an area in which the population has increased 50 per cent in the last generation to have increased its reporting staff substantially, if not 50 per cent. To some extent newspapers have increased their reporting staffs, but meanwhile the work week in the newspaper business has dropped from about 60 hours to 40 hours and even less in many cases. Thus, just to keep even with what it was doing thirty years ago a paper should have increased its staff by one third. If we add to this a population increase, a tenfold increase in the public interest, plus an undetermined amount for mobility, we find that newspapers are woefully understaffed if they are to provide the same kind of coverage of local affairs that they did a generation ago.

Even if we add the reporters to be found in radio and TV stations, the number of reporters covering an area today is far less proportionally than it was thirty or forty years ago.

But this understaffing is more apparent than real. The daily newspaper

[7]

is always reminded that it is in competition for the time of the citizen. The competition for man's time comes not only from radio and TV but more importantly from sports, from do-it-yourself programs, from education, from outboard motors and the golf course. Reader surveys show that most people spend 40 to 45 minutes a day reading the newspaper. At a reading speed of 500 words a minute (which incidentally is much better than most people can do), the fast reader digests 30 or 40 columns a day. Less well-equipped readers fare even more poorly.

A 40-page newspaper contains 320 columns. Much of it to be sure is in the form of comic strips, pictures, advertising layouts, but the so-called news hole in any respectable daily will range every day from 100 columns up—more than twice as much as even the fast reader will cover.

Not only does this pressure affect the news columns alone; it also affects the news which is carried in the advertising columns and which is so vitally important, since most adults devote the major portion of their lives to getting and spending.

Increased circulation and increased attempts to cover the news as circulation areas grow larger means bigger staffs and bigger presses and more equipment. As the newspaper raises its advertising rates to meet these increased costs, one of the first things that happens is that the neighborhood store stops advertising. It is no longer profitable for the store to do so. It draws its trade from the immediate neighborhood, and to continue advertising in the daily and expanded newspaper would mean paying for circulation which never would do the store any good.

Presses and the production of type and the cost of paper and a host of other factors tend to limit the size of a paper which can be produced. Thus there are limits to which a paper can aspire in size, limits both psychological and, of course, economic.

Thus the daily press is confronted with many more times the amount of news it can possibly print and many more times the amount of news which would be read. What it does is to be seen in the treatment of obituaries by papers of various sizes. In the small city of perhaps 30,000 to 50,000, anybody who dies, no matter however humble, will have a story about his death printed in the newspaper. But as the size of the community covered by the newspaper increases to 500,000, the paper becomes selective. A man or woman must have achieved some minor distinction to have his death noted in a story. In short, some people die and their passing is never mentioned in the newspaper. In New York and other great metropolitan centers, a man must have more than a minor distinction to achieve a story about his death. In fact in the tabloids a man must have been a merchant prince, a member of royalty, a gangster, a politician of current responsibilities, or a relative of someone in the newspaper's composing room to achieve the temporary notoriety of having his death noticed in the news columns.

The threshold of attention of daily newspapers and other media everywhere is being raised by the pressure of news propagated by increased population, mobility, and public interest. Great areas of what used to be news, not only in the form of stories about the passing deaths in the community, but the larger areas, concerned with violations of various kinds of laws, are no longer printed.

Although this news is unprinted, the information it contains is still needed and still useful. The citizen has the right to know it. He needs to know it. But much of the daily press is no longer in a position to help him get it. And he is in no position to get it himself.

This impairment of the right to know, brought about not so much by deliberate intent upon the part of any of the participants, but by the very nature of our changing society, has led to many efforts to establish meaningful communications.

A whole generation of scholars, beginning with Korzybski and Ogden and Richards, have attacked the problem semantically. They have been bulwarked by Chase and Thurman Arnold and others, but in the final analysis about all they have been able to do is to warn people that words are not things, and that many words are merely generalities. The warning is fine, and it is useful as far as it goes but a warning to be watchful of the specifics of meaning does not help the average citizen if he has no means of securing knowledge about the specific. The warning is only another generality.

People depending upon their problems have met the necessity for knowing in various ways. In some areas special groups have arisen to meet the need for special information—information which used to be available to the whole community. Organized labor, for instance, has established its own press and a wide network of information agencies to keep its members informed as to its gains, its losses, and its goals. Educational and social welfare organizations, as well as churches, have done much the same.

Business was the first to feel the need for special information not ordinarily available through customary means of communication. For centuries the businessmen of the community who dealt in credit and commercial honesty had, of necessity, to know and to know quickly the credit status of people who wished to use their facilities and with whom they were doing business. From an informal and somewhat disorganized operation this need for credit information grew into the great commercial information centers which are to be found throughout the United States.

In more recent years the breakdown in communications has caused the business community to employ what are called public relations experts in quantities, but in fact these public relations people are essentially communications experts. They use not only the established communication media but they have shown considerable ingenuity in developing new means of communication the essential messages of business to the community of employees and others in whom business is interested.

Because information is so hard for the average citizen to acquire he often adopts the attitude that he will delegate his responsibilities in this connection to some governmental body, to the police to keep order, to the juvenile court to keep the children in line, to the fire department to make sure that he is not living in a firetrap, to the food inspectors to make sure that he is not cheated or poisoned, to the courts to make sure that malefactors are punished, to the schools to make sure that the children are brought up in an orderly fashion.

Evidence of this is to be found in the attitude of metropolitan apartment dwellers who brag about having lived in the same apartment for years and have yet to speak to any of their neighbors. This is fine for the lucky ones, but for the unlucky ones upon whom is visited disaster in the form of theft, or assault, suddenly it becomes terribly important to know about one's neighbors. Here for a moment at least the apartment dweller is faced with a fundamental truth and discovers not that no man is an island, but that no man can be an islander unless he lives on an island. Sometimes, then, the wall of security which money buys and caution guards is breached.

In this circumstance where there is a need and the conventional transmission belts for knowledge are inadequate to the task, it would appear inevitable, considering the climate of opinion, that the government would try to fill that need; that it would in fact try to supply the people with the things that they need in order to know the facts of life as they live them.

To meet this need, the government in fact—not only federal, but state and local—has galloped to the rescue. States have enacted blue sky laws designed to prevent fraud in securities. Local municipalities require that peddlers be licensed and from the license the householder is supposed to infer that the peddler is roughly honest. The national government has enacted the Federal Trade Commission laws which require that food be correctly labeled. It has enacted the Securities and Exchange laws which declare that securities must be accurately described.

This attempt to supply needed information constitutes only one of the directions in which the government has ridden off. Confronted by the pressure for information, by the pressures of tradition, of war, of politics,

[10]

of lobbies, of bureaucracy, and of inertia, the government has ridden off in all directions.

Federal department heads plead with Congress for more money to hire public relations people, while at the same time denying Congress access to information which it needs to legislate. A state attorney general starts a campaign to inform housewives about house-to-house peddlers in order to keep them from being defrauded. At the same time he refuses to tell those housewives whether the cleaning women they hire are also getting relief checks and thus defrauding the state. School boards complain bitterly about a lack of understanding of their problems at the same meeting at which they vote to exclude the public and the press from their deliberations.

But not only is the government engaged in forays and defenses, in charges and countercharges, the whole fabric of government operation—judicial, legislative, and executive—is being rewoven under the impact of the limitations upon what can be known and hence upon the right to know which have been imposed by urbanization.

Since the media of mass communications have not been able to publish all the news that is fit to print, they must choose and select. Therefore, the more prominent the culprit, the more likely stories about him are to find their way into the channels of mass communications. If a banker be accused of drunken driving, his name will be emblazoned in the press, but if the custodian of the bank be accused of the same offense, there will be no mention of it.

The reason for this lies in the fact that there are so many such cases in the larger community that the press, flooded with news, has raised its threshold of attention. In this particular case, the threshold no longer consists of an arrest for drunken driving. There has been the addition of another requirement. The person arrested for this particular offense must be of some prominence.

Thus in a very real sense, population growth and its effects upon the ability of people to know and of the mass media to report make for injustice. Some wrongdoers suffer the penalty imposed by the courts. Others suffer not only the penalty imposed by the court, but an additional penalty of publicity.

Mobility, as well as population growth, operates to make equal justice for all an illusion where the society and the mass media are faced with the difficult communication task inherent in the urbanization of America. The mobility of any person depends upon the strength of his ties to the community in which he lives. These ties may be family, social, financial, and others. They are stronger in persons of substance and less

[11]

strong among the rootless. Thus circumstances compel the person of substance to remain in the community after his arrest and the consequent
unfavorable publicity. It might be thought that the very well-to-do might
escape, because of the mobility of capital, but this, too, is an illusion for
the media of mass communication will pursue them wherever they go.

But the rootless, whose only appearance in the channels of mass
communication has resulted from arrest for crime, readily slide into the
anonymous mass of another neighborhood, or, with a bit more mobility,
into the depths of another city and the increase in the ease of mobility has
made rootlessness attractive to more and more people.

All three classes—the well-to-do, the people of substance, and the
rootless—have paid the penalty exacted by the law. But the rootless
manage to escape from the censorious eyes of the community. The others
cannot do so.

Metropolitan bar associations, and the judges in heavily populated
communities (and it is important to make the distinction between metropolitan members of the bar and others, for attorneys in smaller communities have lived with publicity, printed and otherwise, all of their
lives) argue that publicity in the mass media is a penalty. They maintain
it is a penalty imposed even if a man is found not guilty.

Seeking equal justice for all, they maintain that penalties should be
imposed by the courts and at the discretion of the courts. It is improper
and disorderly for penalties to be imposed by the press which is not a part
of the government and certainly not a part of the judicial machinery
designed specifically to deal with offenders against the law.

This argument is the basis, not only for the secrecy provisions of the
juvenile delinquency and youthful offender statutes, but for laws which
would limit the pretrial publication of news about arrests and for proposals
to limit the reporting of trials themselves.

Such proposals are generally classified as attacks upon the right to
know. They are in fact, although that is not their intention. The end
sought is equal justice for all; the effect upon the right to know is inadvertent. Nevertheless the effect is there and whether the limitations
implicit in such proposals is inadvertent or otherwise, those who are
affected may be expected to continue to fight for their traditional rights.

This example which illustrates how the substantive impairment of the
right to know affects judicial administration also hints at some of the
problems created in the field of law enforcement by the breakdown of
communications, mass and personal.

All societies are governed by law, but government and the law
enforcing agencies are not enough. The smooth and orderly operation
of society depends upon the climate of opinion in that society. And this

[12]

rule applies not merely to the selection of the governors of any society. The voter in a democracy, or the citizen in any society not only needs information upon which to decide for whom to vote. His job is not only to weigh the performance of politicians and vote for them and against them. His job has another and even more important aspect and one which tends to be forgotten—that is, the job of supporting the law.

There is a great deal of talk about the fact that the law will not long continue to be enforced unless it is supported by public opinion. This is a truism, but the function of public opinion in this axiom is seldom examined or defined in any but the vaguest of generalities. The public support of any law must go beyond urging its adoption, beyond resolving to campaign for legislators who will vote for it, beyond expressing approbation of it in letters to congressmen or to the editor, and beyond voting "yes" in a public opinion poll. The truly effective enforcement of the law depends upon the help which the private citizens give to the legal authorities in detecting violations of the law and in apprehending wrongdoers.

Requisite to a willingness to help enforce the law is an understanding and a knowledge of the law. Except in the case of the Ten Commandments and a few other prohibitions, people must be continually reminded of the laws which have been passed to make it possible for millions to live together closely. Thus the Biblical proscriptions, "Thou shalt not kill," and "Thou shalt not steal," are clear and understandable. But it is not so clear to most people why a man is forbidden to install an electrical outlet in his workroom, but must have it done by a certified electrician.

This is not a new concept. It is as old as the organization of human societies and has been identified by Margaret Mead and Machiavelli. The need for the continuous enforcement of the law and for reminding people that the law exists and that help is needed in enforcing the law is stronger than ever and becomes stronger as the population and the public interest grow.

Although the need is greater, the means to meet the need is comparatively weaker. Man is still man bounded by time, by space, and by the mental capacities that he had a thousand years ago. The multitude of laws, the complexity of the public interest, the shadowy parade of new people who leave their impressions on the mind leave but little time for him to help in enforcing the law.

The media of mass communications, deluged by a torrent of news, cannot begin to report all of the happenings which are important to the citizen. They must pick and choose.

This circumstance has had many important effects upon the administration of the law. One of the most dramatic can be described as law enforcement by publicity.

With the media of communications literally unable to print the news of the arrests and convictions of all of those who break all of the laws; with the threshold of attention raised so that only those who are prominent by reasons of wealth, position, or criminal outrageousness will receive space in the media of communications, the law enforcing agencies find themselves in the position of looking for cases to prosecute which will result in publicity, for to enforce the law they need continual notice in the newspapers of the fact that the law exists and that it is being enforced.

This is not a new concept. And as a matter of fact it is practiced in a sophisticated manner by administrative agencies in the federal and state governments. Such organizations as the Internal Revenue Bureau frequently decide which cases to prosecute in terms of which cases will bring the most publicity, or the most publicity for the area in which they are momentarily interested. For instance, some people in the bureau became interested in the lack of income tax returns from waiters and headwaiters. They felt, and probably with some degree of justification, that these men and women around the nation were not reporting as income all of the gratuities that they received. They might well have picked upon the headwaiter in some dive along the St. Louis waterfront, but this would hardly have received nationwide publicity so instead they looked first for the most famous eatery in the nation—one with a nationwide reputation. Then they looked to see if the headwaiter was reporting all of his gratuities. They alleged that he had not and so the headwaiter at the Waldorf-Astoria in New York was arrested and later convicted of withholding some gratuities or of not reporting some portion of his gratuities.

The prosecution had of course two effects. First it convicted a tax evader. But more important than that it served notice on all the waiters, headwaiters, etc. all over the country that the law required them to report gratuities as taxable income. The Income Tax Bureau reports that the amount of taxable income reports by waiters and people in jobs who depend upon gratuities for a large part of their income has increased substantially since the arrest was first made.

The pernicious aspect of this method of enforcing the law is that it does not give equal protection under the law. It lies in the fact that individuals are singled out, not because they are breaking the law any more than anyone else, but because they are prominent. They are in fact penalized for being prominent, not for breaking the law.

This is comparable to the rules of guerilla warfare as imposed by the Nazis and later by the Russians, and decried and legislated against under the rules of international law. Under these rules, the Germans and the Russians were accused again and again of securing some sort of compliance with their rule as conquerer by shooting or killing or threatening to kill the prominent men in every village.

The inability of the communication media to do more than skim the cream from the news has had and is having its effect upon our legislative system, effects which range from the use of congressional committees as reporters to the increasing use of press agents by the congressmen. The most significant effect upon the legislative system is illustrated by what has happened in New York City and to a lesser but growing extent in other great metropolitan centers.

In the days before a congressional election, particularly in a presidential election year, it is difficult to find in the New York City newspapers anything about the candidates of the various parties for the Congress. The city elects some 22 congressmen. While the newspapers will devote columns to the presidential candidates, they will carry, in the whole six weeks preceding the election, only three or four lines devoted to each congressional candidate. This is not done out of malice, or for any sinister purpose; it happens because the newspapers simply do not have the room to report the congressional battles district by district when the area and population which they cover is so large and the population so numerous. A like situation exists in respect to state and local offices in areas outside of New York City.

This news blackout changes or affects our whole traditional system of electing representatives. The Constitution indicates that each representative is to be the spokesman for his district in matters of national concern. But a news blackout of this kind means that for all practical purposes, the candidate for Congress in New York City depends for his election not upon his knowledge of the district which he represents, but rather upon the majority which the national ticket rolls up. He is merely a rider on the national ticket. He wins or loses an election, not because the people in the district know him and like or dislike him, but because the people in his district know the record of the party he represents and like or dislike it.

Since the candidate owes his election to the national party, he takes his guidance from the national headquarters and not from the local district. The situation which obtains is thus roughly comparable to that which exists in England, where in general the people vote for the party and not for the candidate.

Furthermore, in circumstances such as these where the national party is largely the controlling factor in the election or defeat of the New York City candidate, it is only logical that the national party exercise an important role in the selection of the candidates. And its reasons for choosing a candidate to represent a district are hardly the same as those of the district. The national party wants someone to represent the district who will not embarrass the national party. The district wants or should want someone who will speak out for its interests, whether or not these are in accord with what the party nationally seeks.

The situation described in New York City applies to other great metropolitan centers and as the population increases and the press is compelled to raise the threshold of its attention still higher, the tendencies found in the New York area will continue to grow. It is not impossible to foresee the time when the selection of candidates for the Congress will come out of Washington, and only in thinly populated areas, where there remains the possibility of securing some personal rapport with the voters, will representatives of the district be elected. In other areas the representatives will represent not the district but the party, and not the local party, but the national party.

Thus while there is a good deal of loose talk about this being an era of mass communications, it is in fact an era in which the things which need to be communicated have far outrun the carrying capacity of the media of mass communication. They may in fact have increased so enormously that they have outrun the capacity of the receivers—the people—to receive the information which needs to be communicated and which can be communicated if we are to continue to operate our traditional democracy.

Out of this fact and the consequent needs have arisen the present backing and filling, the charges and countercharges over the right to know. From this welter of conflicting aims and purposes will in all probability come not only a new understanding, a new concept of the right to know, but a thorough re-examination of the functions and limitations of the media of mass communications, and a re-examination of our political institutions to recast them in ways which will more nearly meet the problems imposed upon the communications media by population, by mobility, and by the increasing public interest.

II

Daily Newspapers

ROBERT D. MURPHY

NEWSPAPERS ARE SUCH A basic element in our society that we cannot consider their future without pondering the social and political changes in prospect.

World politics and scientific technology do not lend themselves to any real forecasts about events in 2000, but they do make it quite certain that one of three things will have happened by then:

1. Civilization will no longer exist. At last man has, in nuclear explosives, the power to destroy himself.

2. Man will live in a highly regimented society. Decisions, probably for the whole world, will be made by a single group which will have access to and control over all means of finding information and distributing it.

3. Our material civilization and democratic processes will both survive. If this happens we shall have a better democracy than we have today, and this, together with technological progress, will give us a civilization in which men can devote much of their time and strength to creative arts and community betterment.

It is idle to speculate on which of these situations will prevail in 2000. It seems likely that man will eventually be able to control his environment. Whether he can control himself and his fellows is the next problem.

Fortunately for our purposes there is no real need to speculate. Quite obviously newspapers will not exist in the year 2000 if civilization is destroyed. If our second alternative takes form, newspapers as we know them will cease to exist. A single central world authority could no more tolerate free discussion and free flow of information than could the dictatorships of the first half of the century. Most certainly brightly colored information pills would be handed out, perhaps in sheets resembling our present newspapers, but this would be no more a newspaper than is *Pravda* or *Izvestia*.

Clearly then we can speculate on the future of newspapers only in the hope that both civilization and democratic processes will survive.

[17]

If this occurs we can be sure that material civilization and democracy will be much improved versions of the 1958 models. Indeed, to survive the next forty years democratic processes must improve faster in the years just ahead than they have since 1776.

Improvement in the democratic process can come only through rapid improvement in the three basic processes which underlie it: information gathering, information transmission, and more rational methods of resolving our public problems.

We are making progress in all these areas. The question is: Will we improve fast enough?

Signposts point toward a more reasonable, a better informed, and a more literate population in the future.

We know our colleges can expect to double their 1958 enrollment in the late sixties or early seventies. We can expect continuation of present trends toward more training beyond the bachelor's degree. Our technological civilization requires this and we are deeply committed to better training in the humanities and social sciences.

The most compelling factor that will act on newspapers will be the existence of a more reasonable, better informed and more critical group of readers than exists in 1958 for any newspaper.

Other strong influences, too, will mold the newspaper into a new form.

Newspaper coverage habits in 1958 are still set pretty much in the forms established in the last decades of the nineteenth century. Editors traditionally deploy their forces in given places and print as "news" whatever information becomes available there. The police station, the courts, the county building can be depended on to supply their daily quota of "copy," while much more important affairs in other areas may be ignored. When a reporter or an editor makes an occasional foray outside the traditional "beats," the result, if successful, is hailed as "enterprise reporting."

With improved methods of transmitting information it may not be necessary to keep a man at police headquarters all day to write routine stories from the crumbs of information that come his way. Instead, the reporter's talent may be used to perform the creative newsgathering which must be the rule if we have a democratic society in the year 2000.

This, then, will be one of the great changes in newspapers in 2000: editorial staffs will not "cover" places to the extent they do in 1958. Instead they will keep asking, "What do people need to know?" Then they will seek out the answers.

This will result in fewer stories in each day's paper, but a more orderly development of each one. It will result, too, in fewer isolated bits of information out of context.

Closely tied in with this trend toward fewer stories, better developed, will be a different concept of timeliness. This change has been in the making since the turn of the century. In their lusty youth, some newspapers touted the "scoop" and the "beat" as their chief assets in the battle for high readership. Competition for the latest scraps of news rose to ridiculous heights in the Hearst-Pulitzer battles of the 1890's. This trend was on the way out, however, even before radio established itself as a superior purveyor of the latest tidbits of news.

The notion that the latest is the most newsworthy is so much a part of our newspaper tradition that it will probably survive long after the year 2000. To a certain extent it is a valid concept. Certainly a newspaper exists to tell its readers what is new. History books and magazines can tell what happened last year or last week. Overemphasis on the latest, however, has sometimes resulted in the publication of newspapers full of relatively unimportant information about events of the preceding twenty-four hours while they ignored vastly more significant affairs simply because there were no last-minute overt events.

By the year 2000 newspapers will be wholeheartedly devoted to the idea that their job is something more than hurling at their readers the crazy quilt of surface events of the few hours before publication. They will strive to relate the events of yesterday and today into a meaningful pattern to help their readers make sensible preparation for tomorrow.

This change is already under way, with our leading newspapers placing increasing emphasis on background, in team reporting jobs which round up available information on a given subject; in short, on "reporting in depth." The *New York Times* has done this often on a fairly small scale and once in a while on a truly large scale. Examples of the latter are nationwide surveys of political trends preceding the 1956 election and another team study of our national attitudes toward racial integration.

It seems likely that newspapers will devote considerably less of their content to entertainment in the year 2000 than they do in 1958. With increased interest in hard news, the newspapers will return to the activity in which they are really superior—the chronicling of events.

Newspapers cannot compete with magazines in entertainment features —magazines in 2000 will still have the advantage of precious time in which to package their product more attractively. It will be impossible to edit and manufacture every twenty-four hours a product to compete in physical attractiveness and mechanical perfection with a magazine which has a deadline only once a week or once a month.

Television's inherent advantages as an entertainment medium are quite apparent. It would seem that increased mechanical perfection will make it even more effective in the entertainment field. It is likely to capitalize, too, on its ability to make viewers spectators at public events.

Nevertheless, radio will be the only medium which really competes in the news field. Its obvious advantages of immediacy will continue to keep it pre-eminent as a bulletin service.

Newspapers, on the other hand, will still have the major load in carrying information. The serious needs of their society and the more serious interests of their readers will make it unnecessary for them to carry the vast amount of entertainment so common in 1958. Magazines and television are better fitted to this function. Newspapers are better suited to keeping their readers informed. It seems likely that newspapers in the future will carry less information on how to cook, how to diet, how to catch a husband.

The space thus freed will be devoted to better presentation of the news of the day.

What will be the place of the editorial in the year 2000? The day of the "interpretive editorial" may be over by then. This function is gradually being taken over by interpretive news articles. Usually they do a better job than can be done in an interpretive editorial because the writer is on the scene of action and because he frankly relies on reporting techniques, which are the basis for any good interpretive writing.

It seems likely that editorials will be used less frequently. Some 200 newspapers in 1958 have no regular space devoted to editorials. It is likely that this number will increase. Editorials will appear when the editor has opinions to express. This is the basic purpose of the editorial. In the need to fill a given amount of space every day many editorial writers have become interpreters of the news, moralists, entertainers or what have you. Probably local material of this type will continue to appear in newspapers of the future, but it will appear under more appropriate headings.

Editorials, when they do appear, will have more effect because they will be less common.

Will new printing processes materially alter the nature of newspapers? It seems unlikely that the newspapers of the year 2000 will be as flossy as the slick magazines. Color printing will certainly be much more common, but the speed with which the contents of a newspaper have to be assembled will forever keep it from being produced as attractively or organized as well as it could be done if the editors and printers had more time. Printing processes may be more efficient, but it is doubtful that they will be any cheaper since labor is such an important factor in the cost of manufacturing a newspaper.

One of the most intriguing areas of speculation about the future of newspapers is in the number of newspapers there will be. Will there be more or less newspaper competition? Will newspapers be bigger units of business or smaller? Will advertising pay more or less of the bill?

Many factors affect this, but three are most important:

1. technological and economic considerations which determine the optimum size of an operation;
2. population trends;
3. the attitude of government.

Ever since the Industrial Revolution machinery for mass production has increased in size and cost. This means that a business involving manufacturing must reach a certain minimum size before it can be efficient. Newspapers are no exception. There is little indication that new machinery will make it feasible for daily newspapers to operate at a profit in the future with smaller circulations than they can in 1958. A projection of trends of the first half of the century would indicate that units may have to become larger, but it may well be that this trend is leveling off.

One of the "cold type" processes was widely heralded in the early 1950's as a means of cutting production costs so that more daily newspapers would be feasible. Toward the end of the decade, however, it had not lived up to its billing, although it did cut down considerably the initial equipment costs of starting a new newspaper.

There seems little in the technological picture to indicate that production costs will really drop to significantly increase the number of daily newspapers. We can hope for better printing and more efficient shops, but these gains will probably be offset by increasing labor costs. This conclusion must remain tentative, however, as technological advances have so often confounded would-be prophets.

Another cost factor is likely to discourage any spectacular increase in the number of dailies. A minimum editorial staff is necessary. As readers become critical enough to demand higher quality newspapers the news staff will increase in size and quality and thus in cost. This will be another economic brake on an increase in the number of dailies.

Our population by the year 2000 is expected to reach 282 million, roughly a 65 per cent increase over the 170-odd million of 1958. Such a population increase, however, does not necessarily point to a similar 65 per cent increase in the number of daily newspapers, 1,755 in 1958. The best opinion is that our population will continue to gravitate to established metropolitan areas, so we cannot expect the number of our population centers to increase materially. Only an increase in the number of population centers would indicate that we will have more daily newspapers. A newspaper needs a population center which is the hub of a trading area since the paper depends on advertising for a major source of its revenue.

This concept of the newspaper as an integral part of a trading center is basic to any predictions as to the number of newspapers in the future. In a very rough sense we need and can support at least as many newspapers as we have trading centers of a certain minimum size. Some trading centers can support more than one daily newspaper, but this number has been steadily decreasing through the middle years of the twentieth century. Rising production costs have reduced more and more communities to the status of one-newspaper towns. It is doubtful that this trend will reverse, although there are signs that it is slowing considerably.

In a study published in *Journalism Quarterly* in 1954, Dr. Raymond B. Nixon predicted no great change in the number of dailies in the following twenty years. Here is his conclusion:

> Finally, the most significant changes in trends since 1945 seem to be (1) a rise in the size of cities where the tendency is toward only one daily, because of spiraling cost, and (2) the attainment of an apparent equilibrium between suspensions and the establishment of new dailies, bringing to an end the long-time trend toward fewer papers nationally. Barring another major social upheaval, the total number of dailies in the United States should not fall much below the present figure, but should rise slowly as more of the growing small cities come of daily size.
>
> Although the daily newspaper publishing industry has had its share of perplexing economic problems in these postwar years, it is in better condition than many other businesses because of the essential nature of the product it has to sell. Indeed, except for a few "marginal papers"—that is, those in cities too small to support a daily, or those in larger cities with excessive competition for the same kind of readers—there is unmistakable evidence that the industry has attained the highest degree of stability in its history.

The attitude of the government has not materially influenced the number of newspapers in the past, but it is likely to be increasingly important. This attitude is most clearly expressed in the enforcement of the antitrust laws in relation to newspapers.

The government first used the antitrust laws directly in relation to newspapers with the *Lorain Journal* case, which came to the United States Supreme Court in 1951. This was an attempt to regulate advertising and certain news practices in connection with radio competition. In St. Louis and New Orleans attempts were made to regulate advertising practices in relation to newspaper competition. In Kansas City the government forced the *Kansas City Star,* which faced no important newspaper competition, to sell its radio station.

It takes little imagination to see in this progression of cases an attempt by the Antitrust Division of the Department of Justice to build up a series of decisions which would make possible increasing regulation of advertising procedures and competitive practices. There was no noticeable change in the Division's policy with the change from a Democratic to a Republican administration after the election of President Eisenhower in 1952.

This trend is likely to continue and the federal courts seem friendly toward it. The Justice Department sustained a major defeat in the St. Louis case but even here it was apparent that the court gave much weight to the fact that the government had failed, in the court's opinion, to prove that the competitive newspaper was actually damaged by the practices the government sought to halt. The victory of the government in the Kansas City case in 1955 is also significant since it succeeded in getting the courts to hold in violation of the provisions of the statute the *Kansas City Star,* a venerable and highly respected newspaper institution.

The over-all effect of the antitrust cases might, under other circumstances, be expected to increase, or at least maintain the number of newspapers at their current level. It seems doubtful, however, that this type of government action will do more than slow the trend toward fewer newspapers. It is likely to make a publisher hesitant to purchase a rival newspaper and merge it with his operation and it may succeed in limiting competitive practices so that a few of the financially weaker newspapers can survive. On the other hand, the forces tending toward bigness are strong, and government action, so far at least, has offered no major counter move to them. It has just made things a little more uncomfortable for the larger newspapers which have resulted from mergers.

Government attitude as expressed in the antitrust prosecutions of newspapers may have an indirect effect in discouraging the development of large chains or groups of newspapers under the same ownership. Newspaper chains expanded rapidly through the first third of the twentieth century, then pretty much stood their ground. By the mid-1950's the country had few expanding chains.

One of the reasons for this was that newspapers in general were making smaller profits in the early 1950's than in previous lush economic periods. Many publishers had not raised advertising and circulation rates to match the increasing costs of production. This made additional units less attractive to chain owners.

There seems little reason to expect that this trend will change. With increased public service expected of newspapers and with a more literate public making it less possible to capitalize on sensational news, newspaper publishing seems less likely to attract in the future the type of owner who regards it primarily as a venture to be entered from profit motives. The man with capital will be able to find more attractive ways to invest his money if profit is his primary motive. There is likely to be some increase in existing chains and groups, but it is doubtful that chains will control a great many more newspapers than they do in 1958. Dr. Nixon, in a 1955 article, concludes that the number of chains or groups is likely to increase, but that each group will be smaller and that we will have mostly regional groups with much local autonomy.

It seems likely that additions to chains will be made primarily by publishers who pick up a newspaper property because they see a genuine opportunity to perform a public service and because they think they can turn it into a profitable business. The opportunity to purchase this kind of property in the next forty years will come less frequently than it has in the first half of the century. There are fewer cities with two or more newspapers, and in many of the communities which have two newspapers one owner already controls both.

Two other factors here will influence the number of newspapers: (1) the tendency for one newspaper to cover two or three adjacent cities and (2) the trend for competing newspapers to merge their business departments, but maintain separate corporations which independently control the news and editorial policies. It is obvious that the first points toward fewer dailies, the second toward more. Both of these trends are so new in the late 1950's that it is impossible to form an opinion as to their long-term effect.

It seems likely that weekly publications will assume more importance in filling coverage gaps left by the big dailies. As the dailies become larger it becomes less possible for them to cover local details in surrounding villages and towns. Most of these places are not large enough to support dailies, but probably could support vigorous weeklies. The daily-weekly combination might give the reader adequate coverage of general news and items of interest only in his immediate area.

Most thoughtful observers expect that in the years ahead we will live in an increasingly regulated society. Government functions seem to increase almost without regard to the wishes of the persons running them. Our citizens expect more and more services and increased government protection. As our population increases and crowds more and. more into our metropolitan areas, increasing regulation seems to be inevitable, whether we like it or not.

It is rather absurd to think that newspapers will be able to escape this increasing amount of government regulation. The question is: Will the newspapers be able to maintain their vigor and editorial independence while submitting to this increased regulation?

What areas of regulation will affect newspapers?

General regulations which affect all business will certainly be applied to newspapers. These include labor regulations, taxes, fair trade practices, rules of fair competition, and many others.

We have already considered the effect of the antitrust regulations. The Sherman Act is a general law, but in its applications to newspapers it could conceivably have a material effect on newsgathering and dissemination. Justice Frank Murphy of the United States Supreme Court was concerned with this danger in his dissenting opinion in the Associated Press case in 1945. The dangers he foresaw did not materialize, but this does not mean that the antitrust laws could not be a threat to the free flow of news. It is conceivable that they could be construed to control the methods of newsgathering and threaten our traditional concept of freedom of the press. On the other hand, these laws could be a positive force in maintaining freedom of information if they make possible the existence of more newspapers and more press associations.

Government administrators in the year 2000 will probably dislike criticism from the press as much as ever. Yet the right to criticize will be just as vital. If the government does loom as a more important agency in regulating the public and in performing more services, how will this affect its relations with newspapers?

More functions and more responsibilities will obviously make it a better news source so that we can expect that more and more news stories will have some kind of governmental tie-in.

More regulatory functions will mean that government will control more of the activities of the citizen's everyday life and therefore it will have considerably more power. Included in the general increase in power will be the means of exerting more direct and indirect control over the contents of the newspapers.

In 1958 the sphere of governmental activity is already so large that a major problem of newspaper reporters is keeping open the channels of information about the government. The question is, with more power and activity can we expect a government to be more responsive to the information needs of readers and therefore more cooperative with newspaper reporters?

The natural tendency of an administrator is to stamp "top secret" on any document within reach. This saves trouble and possible embarrassment just in case the document should somehow show that government made a mistake. That human nature will force the retention and enlargement of this tendency seems inevitable. This is a serious problem in 1958. It will be more serious still if government activities continue to increase.

It is safe to say that newspapers will be quite ineffective by the year 2000 unless some new means have been devised by then to make the general run of government information freely available to every private citizen—including, of course, newspaper reporters. Presumably this would make the administrator assume the burden of proving why a document should be kept secret. Enforcement would have to be in the hands of some impartial agency—perhaps the courts.

Some sort of system for this purpose will have to exist in the year 2000 or our newspapers will be unable to perform the function demanded of a free press in a free society.

What of the people who will write and edit our country's newspapers in the year 2000?

Better quality newspapers will require better quality staffs. Less routine news will mean less room for routine reporters. In the future nearly every reporter will have to be as good as today's best.

Newspapers are becoming aware that their greatest asset is a high quality staff. Some newspapers are insisting on adequate training. Some give leaves for further study, and a few fellowships are available for study in this country or abroad. It seems likely that the development of a high caliber staff will be a primary consideration of many publishers of the future. To compete for the time of better informed readers, newspapers will have to select potentially superior writers and editors and then encourage them to develop their highest talent.

To achieve a better staff publishers will have to plow back a larger amount of a newspaper's profit into editorial department salaries. But salaries are only a part of the picture. What is more important is that superior achievement will have to be recognized, and reporters encouraged and expected to do superior work.

There is nothing revolutionary in this. Our best newspapers are doing it in 1958. It will mean that newspaper workers will have the same prestige in their community that is accorded to other professionals. There is nothing revolutionary in this, either. Good reporters in 1958 have as much prestige as anyone could desire.

Reporters and editors of 2000 will have all the techniques and the sensitivity of the social scientists, plus the skill to interpret day-to-day events against this background.

What will be the responsibilities of the newspapers in the year 2000? That is easy. They will be the same as those already upheld by our best newspapers. These are simply recognition that the newspaper's real reason for existence is telling its readers what they need to know in such a way that readers can understand it and apply it to themselves.

To do this newspapers of the future will have the use of many refined research techniques. They will be able to determine easier what is on their readers' minds and so respond more quickly to it. These same research techniques will make available many more stories than are used today about the readers themselves. Political trends will be spotted earlier, for example. In many other ways newspapers will find that often their readers are their best stories.

In order to hold their more enlightened readers of the future newspapers will have to be more enlightened still. It is not too much to expect that newspapers of the year 2000 will know their readers' best interests just a little better than even their readers know them; and that newspapers will be an even stronger force for reason and understanding.

III

The Weekly Newspaper

HOWARD W. PALMER and GENE GILMORE

THE WEEKLY NEWSPAPER WILL CONTINUE to flourish throughout the twentieth century. Its character will change, its influence will increase, and its quality will improve. The weekly, in many cases, will give far more attention to civic and cultural affairs than will the big city daily. A greater number of the weeklies will become highly literate papers, devoted to the progress of the community. Many publishers will note the intellectual growth of the small towns and their papers will become better looking and better edited.

These changes will take place despite a growth of suburban and rural coverage by city dailies. Radio and television, on the other hand, will never offer serious competition to the weekly newspaper.

Weeklies will make these gains while shrinking in numbers. Some new papers will start but even more will fail. The paper now tottering on the edge of bankruptcy, in many instances, will go over the brink. Papers located in hamlets, hemmed in by larger towns with strong weeklies, will be forced out. This is a trend that has been evident for the last forty years. In towns where there are now two newspapers, there will be only one. Business will simply be inadequate for two strong weekly papers. And unless the weekly of the future is strong, with good circulation, good news coverage, and modern business practices, it will be in danger of failing.

New weeklies will be born in the suburban areas of our large cities and, in some cases, within the cities themselves. The normal growth of population will bring a steady expansion of suburbs. Little towns in the shadow of the big city will suddenly become communities of 10,000 people. Whole new semimetropolitan areas will be created. Community interests in these new little cities will demand a newspaper. The person with a little capital, a fair amount of credit, some newspaper experience, and business skill will find a market for a weekly paper in such communities.

The person dreaming of owning his own suburban weekly would be wise to realize that the suburbs probably will not grow in size in the coming years as they have in the dozen years following World War II. Some evidence is available to show that many families, after their children are grown, are willing to return to the city where commuting is not a problem and where outstanding cultural and social events are easily available.

It seems likely, too, that population in the United States will not go up three million every year until the year 2000. The fluctuations in where people locate and how fast the human race increases will have to be judged with care by anyone thinking of establishing a weekly paper.

The bulk of population growth probably will be in the medium and large cities. Even during the population boom following 1940, the small country town, as a rule, has not increased rapidly in population. The big cities and their suburbs, however, have burgeoned. Despite much talk about decentralization of industry, most new factories and businesses have located in the bigger cities. Transportation has been better, the labor market more flexible, and executives generally have preferred living in metropolitan areas. This trend is almost certain to continue.

Prospects are good for a small paper functioning within the heavy circulation area of the giant dailies. Most of our big cities are divided into communities, many of them with names almost as common to residents as the big city itself. Many weeklies already have been started in these areas and have prospered. Their formula is rather simple. They print the news that interests the people in their community. The big daily cannot be so exclusive in its coverage. It must cover the world and Washington, the state capitol and city hall. The daily cannot afford to cover in detail the news of interest only to a small region.

Dailies have exerted much energy in covering suburban areas and can be expected to extend this coverage. Their efforts, however, are usually incomplete, by necessity, and fail to give the reader the sense of identification he gets when reading a paper solely devoted to the news of his own area.

Some of the weeklies in the larger small towns will become dailies. Most weekly publishers, however, will be reluctant to make the shift. They realize the switch will mean that their new daily will be small, with low circulation as dailies go. Expenses, at the same time, will jump while incomes will not go up materially. Many publishers, faced with the proposal of going daily, will reply, "Why should I change from a strong weekly to a very small daily?" This is the alternative many will face but most weekly publishers will not launch a daily until they are certain the community will support it. Many well-meaning citizens in a smaller town will urge the establishment of a daily. Their arguments in favor of such an enterprise can be expected to be based on ego satisfaction—they think it would flatter their town to have a daily paper.

Those weeklies in cities that possibly warrant dailies may be wise to start publishing twice a week. A few such papers now dot the nation and the number may increase. Some publishers, aiming for daily operation, have gone from weekly to twice a week to three times weekly. Then they make the plunge to a five-day-week daily. They plan no expansion beyond the five-day schedule. This gradual change has many advantages. The shift can be accomplished with less turmoil. The readers get adjusted to getting the paper more often than once a week. And, most of all, the publisher has not taken a giant step until he is sure the short steps are going to work.

Twice-weekly papers may crop up in cities too big for a weekly and not quite big enough for a daily. They may arrive, too, in a rather small community but with a large agricultural area around it—one that is prosperous and capable of yielding enough advertising to make twice-weekly production profitable. These papers may find it hard to get enough local news to fill two papers weekly and will take on a limited wire service. The essentials of world and state news can be contained in their paper this way and whenever local news is short there will be a ready supply of copy.

The main drawback to twice-weekly production will be the facts of advertising life. Grocery store advertising makes up a good sized part of any weekly's advertising income. These stores only want to advertise on Thursday, to tap the big week-end market. Going into a twice-weekly paper will mean that the Thursday paper will be the money-maker and the Tuesday paper a loser. Publishing Friday instead of Thursday generally will be opposed by the advertiser. And publishing Monday instead of Tuesday for the other half of the week's output will bring serious news-gathering problems since it is so close to the week end.

So most weeklies will continue as weeklies, even when published in fairly good-sized towns. The owners will know that their product is good and the paper produces a good profit. They will know it is well-read and respected. The readers are satisfied and so are the advertisers. Publishers of such papers will declare that they are content to publish a good paper once a week. Increasing the number of issues, in their opinion, will bring additional problems with little more revenue.

Radio no longer offers much news competition to any newspaper, daily or weekly. Television offers dailies some competition and, like radio, has brought some changes in daily newspaper operation. The elimination of the newspaper "extra" is an example of how radio and TV have altered the handling of news by newspapers.

Radio, at one time, made a slight dent in weekly newspaper coverage. Television will not make the slightest impression. Nearly all TV stations are in good-sized cities. They cannot report anything but the barest details of small town or community happenings. The TV newscast must consist of items of almost universal interest. Otherwise the listener will switch stations. The newspaper can be filled with news items which individually attract only a minority of readers. But each minority can be satisfied. Each reader can be his own editor. What he does not want to read he can pass over. Once tuned to a TV news show, the listener can't say to the announcer, "No, I'm not interested in that item. Skip it."

Some of the best examples of good weekly suburban newspapers can be found in the areas surrounding New York and Chicago. Some of these function right in Manhattan itself, such as the *Town & Village,* serving approximately 100,000 people in the east side of 14th Street, and the *Village Voice,* a newspaper printing the news of Greenwich Village. More than two dozen weeklies flourish in Long Island, several of them being actually still in the city of New York. The *Times* of Ridgewood, which is a part of the city of Brooklyn, has more than 10,000 paid circulation. Within the suburban area, with large circulation, are the *Huntington Long Islander,* the *Great Neck News,* and the *Great Neck Record,* while at the end of the Island are two nationally known, prize-winning newspapers, the *Patchogue Advance* and the *Riverhead News-Review.*

The Paddock Publications put out thirteen weeklies in the suburban areas of Chicago. The papers are printed in one plant and to some extent the same editorial and advertising material is usable in all thirteen. More such chain operations in suburban regions are likely.

Only a few of the new weeklies will result from the coming of age of the little advertising sheet, often called a shopper. These cheaply produced papers often start adding a little news to enhance their readership. But when they gradually shift into full-fledged community newspapers with paid circulation, they often falter. Their readers are unwilling to pay for something they previously got free. In a few cases, the shopper can be converted into a fine-looking, profitable weekly newspaper. This is rare, however.

The weekly publisher who succeeds in the rural community will need more than ability. He will require a fairly prosperous region, prosperous in agriculture, industry or both. He will be greatly helped if he does not have a strong competing weekly only a few miles away. His business future will be about as promising, generally, as the business future of the town itself. If most of the residents shoot off to a neighboring city to do their buying, it is almost certain the newspaper will have financial difficulty. The merchant with little income will not be able to advertise. And advertising is the financial heart of any paper, daily or weekly. It can also be said that a weekly publisher will have extra problems if the spirit of the town is poor. A community that is apathetic, bored, or pessimistic will be a tough place to run a paper.

Yet many an editor in the past has taken over a run-down paper in a sluggish town and revived both the paper and the town. There is no reason to believe that this will not be done in the future. In fact, the ambitious person with little capital will have more opportunities to have his own newspaper by purchasing a paper that has been poorly managed. The price of such a paper is usually low, yet the potential may be high. An energetic person may be able, after great effort, to spruce up the paper and promote civic interest until commercial opportunities in the town are healthy. This kind of work takes a combination of peculiar talents and tremendous toil, but some will have what it takes.

Given a proper geographical location, the weekly editor of the future will prosper and have great influence in a community. He will require three main talents: Being a good reporter himself, understanding business methods as they pertain to printing and publishing, and having a personality that will blend well with the people in his town.

The weekly of the future is going to have to be filled with news. It will have to be attractive typographically. It will have to provide helpful advertising services. It will have to be promoted. And, most of all, the successful publisher will have to use modern accounting and bookkeeping. An editor may be a whiz with the news, a genius with makeup, and an advertising giant, but if he is unable to have an efficient business operation he is doomed to mediocrity or failure.

The day is quickly fading in which a reporter could buy a weekly paper and succeed in putting out a fine edition without knowing how to cut costs and improve efficiency. At the same time, the printer, who knows his way around a composing room so well, will be unable to do well in the newspaper business unless he also understands how to report the news so people will buy his paper.

The publisher of the future will have to be a jack-of-all trades within the newspaper business and a master of at least most of them. Ideally, he will be a combination reporter, editor, advertising salesman, layout man, bookkeeper, cost accountant, tax expert, printer, pressman, editorial writer, circulation man, and efficiency expert. No person, of course, can be skilled in all these fields. The successful weekly publisher, however, will have a basic understanding of all of them and be able to employ capable persons to perform the key jobs of his enterprise.

To keep these capable employees, he will have to treat them fairly and pay them good salaries. He will have to approach business propositions coldly and with great care. One serious mistake may cost him the profits of several years.

This future publisher also will have to be willing to work hard and long, particularly in the years while the paper is being established or while the mortgage is being paid off. The forty-hour week will not apply to him in his early years and, for that matter, probably never will.

The publisher in a small town will have to have a genuine affection for farmers, factory workers, and small businessmen if he is to attain maximum success. The ultrasophisticate, the snob, or the person who does not enjoy life in a small town has no place in the country weekly.

The weekly in years to come generally will avoid being the organ of a political party. The number of "political" papers is declining steadily. The independent voter is coming into his own and will demand that the news of all political groups be printed fairly. At the same time, the growing number of ticket-splitting voters will demand that the editorials be written with an air of independence. Slavish devotion to one party on the editorial page is really not much better than slanting the news in the rest of the paper. The reader, to be interested in the editorial page, will expect to find reasoned presentation of opinion, even if he disagrees with it. If the editorial page is a labored and repetitious defense of one political group, the publisher can expect to have little influence.

The editorial page of the future, far more than in the past, will have to stress logic, amusement, and humor. When an issue boils within a community, the paper will have to exhibit a staunchness, a backbone that will permit the printing of the news and opinion without fear. An editor will be poorly regarded in his town if he runs from a fight. And his influence will be decreased if, in this fight, he is not fair with those who disagree with him or if he lets his emotions run wild in print. The power of the press still is great and the abuse of that power will lead to distrust or open hostility by the public.

Photography is certain to play a much bigger role in the weekly newspaper of tomorrow. More newsmen will be able to take suitable pictures and press cameras and darkrooms will be common in weekly paper offices. The better weeklies today are making good use of pictures and in years to come nearly all of them will make pictures an important part of their journalism.

The development of electronic engraving devices has been amazing in recent years. These machines can either be rented or bought and some weeklies already have secured this equipment. Their engravings are good and public reaction to the abundance of pictures has been exceptional. The weekly of the future may consider its engraving machine as indispensable as a linotype. In any case, it is almost certain that by 1975, say, no weekly will be far from a place where quick and inexpensive electronic engraving is available. It will be a rare weekly publisher who fails to make full use of such equipment. This machine will be as valuable an adjunct to the advertising department as it is to the news side. Many an advertising manager will be able to increase lineage if he can offer low-cost engravings to a space buyer.

Chain operations in country papers probably will decline. In the suburban areas, however, it is likely that one publisher will stretch out until he is publishing several papers. The country papers, in chains, have found in recent years that it is often more profitable to publish one strong weekly than to put out two or three little ones. This trend can be expected to continue.

But where it is possible to have several strong weeklies in a certain highly populated area, it is almost certain that chain operations will be extended. All of them can be printed in one plant. A high-speed press will be capable of turning out a weekly circulation in little more than an hour. This centralized plant will be able to afford a highly efficient composing room. The plant will be equipped to set type and print for a half-dozen or more papers.

With such an operation, of course, it will be essential to have a large job printing department that will provide work for employees and machinery whenever they are not busy getting out newspapers. Most weeklies are printed for Wednesday or Thursday publication and most of the mechanical work on them is done in the first three days of the week. It will be important for a chain publisher to find work that will keep his expensive presses running more than one day a week.

Many weeklies will expand a great deal in the coming years, both in circulation and size of editions. Most presses in weekly papers now print only eight pages at a time. Many of them are already printing two, three, or even four sections running as high as thirty-six pages. These sections have to be put together by hand and the labor costs on this job are high. Often printers making $2.50 an hour are drafted for the work. As papers grow and circulation climbs, these costs are going to multiply. A paper of 3,000 circulation now may very well reach a figure twice that in fifteen or twenty years. The problem that will face many publishers in years to come will be space and equipment. Where and how can they print that many papers economically without buying a new plant and costly new equipment?

Many of them will answer that question this way: They will turn their present plants into job printing shops and set their own newspaper type and advertising. They will install a mat roller and make impressions of their pages on mat paper. The mats then can be taken some distance, if necessary, to a plant where, for a price, type plates will be made and high speed presses used. The number of pages printed at one time this way is unlimited, so far as a weekly is concerned. This weekly editor will let someone else worry about keeping the press busy all week. He'll occupy it for a couple hours, paying far less in the long run than if he had installed the expensive equipment himself.

The improvement of highways in coming years should facilitate this trend. Within a few hours a truckdriver could take mats to a city even fifty miles way, have several thousand copies of a paper printed, and be back home with the finished product ready for distribution. The total time would be little more than required to print on the old-style press the publisher has by-passed.

It would not even be engaging in Buck Rogers fantasy to propose that a rented helicopter could fly the mats to the high-speed plant and fly the papers back, possibly within two hours time.

Weekly newspapermen looking to the future occasionally suspect that a revolution in printing processes is about to erupt. Some even foresee the day when the composing room force will be gone, and that in the place of printers and pressmen will be one man who pushes buttons—and calls a repairman when something goes wrong.

Such astounding progress seems only a dream. It is true that new printing processes, largely photographic, are in use and have reduced, to some extent, the reliance on manpower. But in each of the cases where this new equipment has been installed the effects are not revolutionary. A saving of 5 per cent in labor may be made on one operation with one new machine. Ten per cent may be saved in another operation by using another machine. But in no case, since the invention of the linotype, have printing costs been cut in half by any device. It should be added that the newest photographic machinery in the printing field is tremendously expensive and the small paper would find it difficult to buy it in the first place. The small paper also would be unable to use it twenty-four hours a day. Without heavy use, the purchase of this costly equipment often could not be justified.

The weekly press of the future, as it has in the past, will lag behind the dailies in the use of new machinery. Country and weekly papers will not be able to afford to experiment. Once the equipment is tested fully and its applications to the weekly field are clear, the successful publisher will be quick to obtain it. Costs of labor are going upward and the only way these higher costs can be met without frequent increases in circulation and advertising rates is to increase the productivity of the mechanical departments by using the most modern equipment.

The job printing departments of weekly newspapers can be expected to continue as a key part of the business. In most cases now, the printing income makes up a minor but important share of the paper's gross income. The publisher couldn't live without it. If the weekly owner pays close attention to his costs, makes sure he is working for a profit, and if he can give quick and good service, the job printing part of a weekly newspaper will remain profitable.

The financial rewards of the weekly editor should rise steadily through the years. Most of these editors now make from $5,000 to $15,000 a year. Perhaps, a handful make as much as $25,000. These incomes, barring serious and long depression, are almost certain to rise. The country editor works long hours and works hard. But when the financial rewards are compared to what he would make as an employee of a daily paper it is clear that the country publisher is doing well.

The rewards other than financial are not so hard to count either. The satisfaction of owning and publishing one's own paper is great today and will remain great. The realization that this is *his* paper, despite the great contributions of others to the finished product, is a feeling that cannot be duplicated in many jobs. The opportunity to contribute to the general welfare, to be a force for good in a community is vast. Few people outside the newspaper business have such a chance. Most weekly publishers take quiet pride in the contributions they have made to their communities. The weekly man knows well that in a big city his voice would count for little. But in his village he is a pillar and he will remain so through the years.

One other reward rates top billing among weekly newspapermen outside the suburbs. This reward comes in the form of room—elbow room. His house may be within a few blocks of the plant, but he has the room and grass and flowers that the New Yorker rides twenty-five miles a day to get. A lake often is only a few minutes drive away and the trout stream no farther. Nature is close to him and he can rub shoulders with it daily. The coming years won't take that away from him.

The weekly newspaper of the future is going to be well edited, interesting, and informative. It will be more alive to its responsibilities than the average weekly today. It will provide more services to the reader and advertiser. Publishers will realize that the small-town resident is not a homespun, unschooled person interested only in gossip about his neighbors. The weekly newspaperman in the years to come will know that many of his readers are well traveled and well educated. He will know that they are as aware, in many cases, of social change and civic progress as their big-city friends. The weekly publisher of the future will recognize these changes. He will be prepared to turn out an attractive, responsible paper, alert to the needs of the twentieth century and willing to help prepare people for the twenty-first.

IV

The Future of Broadcast Journalism

EUGENE S. FOSTER

The Challenge

> So much man has accomplished. As he faces the future, he holds
> in one hand the key to universal understanding, in the other a
> fragment of nuclear energy, so awesomely destructive that none
> would dare to loose it, save through misunderstanding. History will
> record how man reacts to this providential coincidence.

These lines were penned over ten years ago as an introduction to a
consideration of radio's role in American society. They antedated television
but are, if possible, even more appropriate to the newer medium. In asses-
sing the future of broadcast journalism, it appears logical to start with this
reference to the proved ability of radio and television as media of communication and to the frightening possibilities inherent in our "progress"
in forging the machineries of conflict.

Just as there is material in a newspaper or magazine which can not be
classified as journalistic, so is it inappropriate to include everything on the
air in the category of broadcast journalism. It is obvious that a "western,"
be it adult or otherwise, or a variety program or a quiz program cannot
claim to further the long tradition of the press. On the other hand, it would
be unduly restrictive to include only those programs which are labeled
newscasts, documentaries or analyses. Rather, it seems appropriate in the
context of this volume to consider broadcast journalism as the attempt of
the broadcaster to use his facilities to meet the challenge presented above.

If history is to record that man reacted adequately to the problems of
today, it is essential that every medium of communication do its share in
educating its audience. The greater the audience, the greater the responsibility. For the broadcaster this obligation implies the airing of programs
which adequately report the daily news and, through on-the-spot coverage

and other techniques, enable the public to learn more about its environment; feature programs which analyze in depth current problems; discussion programs which present all points of view on controversial issues, and
programs which provide leadership of public opinion. This, then, is the
specific challenge in broadcast journalism for the licensee of broadcast
facilities.

Broadcasting's Unique Character

Broadcasting is unique among the media of communication in its
usage of resources which are at once public property and inherently limited
in quantity. The individual or company wishing to start a new newspaper
or magazine is free to do so if he has sufficient funds. Even during war
years when there is a shortage of labor or of material such as newsprint,
he is welcome to enter the market place and bid against established com-
petitors for whatever is necessary and available.

On the other hand, the potential broadcaster must go to a government
regulatory board for permission to use the air waves, knowing they are
limited and have been established as the property of the people. Frequently,
he will find there is no room in the spectrum for his radio or television
station and no amount of money or political influence can expand the air
waves to accommodate him.

The American system of radio regulation is nearly as old as broadcasting itself, which had been only seven years in existence when the
Federal Radio Act of 1927 was signed into law. The subsequent passage of
the Federal Communications Commission was not significant in the history
of broadcasting because it simply placed the provisions of the 1927 law in
the context of sections dealing with the other media of mass communications.

The Federal Communications Commission has, among its other
duties, the obligation to regulate radio-television broadcasting in "the public
interest, convenience and necessity." Implementation of that responsibility
involves the issuance and denial of licenses and rule-making with regard
to broadcasting. No one may operate a transmitter without specific permission of the Commission and without first signing a waiver to any claim on
ownership of the frequency whose usage he seeks.

In effect, the procedure of licensing limited facilities establishes a
quasi-monopoly for those who are fortunate or foresighted enough to
first seek permission to broadcast. In the early days of the Radio Act, the
monopoly kept the number of stations down to the point that there were
very few which were marginal and unable to survive on the advertising
dollars available. The Commission at that time had extremely stringent
technical standards protecting the signals of existing stations and equally

stringent financial criteria which prevented new stations which might cause economic injury to those already on the air.

In the early days radio was permitted, like Topsy, "to just grow." In any given section of the country it was a matter of "first come-first served." As long as frequencies were available, they were assigned to the major communities where the commercial potential was first evident.

Since 1952 the Federal Communications Commission has been giving television licenses on a predetermined plan which reserved channels for smaller markets. Such reservation has severely limited the number of stations in some metropolitan areas. The effect of a government-granted monopoly has been heightened by the economic failure of the ultra high frequency stations.

For example, one of the country's half dozen largest markets has only three very high frequency television stations. In 1957 one of them was sold as part of a package which cost $20 million. Of this amount $12,600,000 was the announced payment for the purchase of the television station exclusive of "land, buildings and other real property." In effect, the purchaser paid over $12 million for a piece of paper from the Federal Communications Commission stating that he was entitled to use one of only three VHF stations which would ever be established in that city.

From this protection of existing stations have come major strengths and major weaknesses of American broadcasting.

Of some significance has been the economic protection of the licensee which has enabled him to spend major amounts of money on things he has deemed most important. Radio and television have been most successful in judging the entertainment desires of the American public. That success has, in part, been due to the fact that the broadcaster has been able to spend millions of dollars annually measuring audience tastes and preferences and on experimentation with program types.

During the war years from 1939 through 1945 radio carried a major burden in the dissemination of news. Citizens at home were able to keep up with events as they occurred all over the world and to hear on-the-spot descriptions which lent far more authenticity than could the printed word. Costs of maintaining news staffs far exceeded the amounts sponsors paid for specific broadcasts but could be easily absorbed by a businessman who knew that new competition could not cut into his profits in the foreseeable future.

Some of the most successful broadcasts in history were the coverage of the national political conventions. The citizen could, as never before, feel that he was participating by viewing his television screen. Yet, each of the three major networks expects to lose several millions of dollars on convention coverage every four years because it pays out far more than it can hope to recover from the sponsors.

In many ways, the program fare of American broadcasting has been immeasurably strengthened from the protection afforded by the fact that the radio spectrum is so limited.

On the other hand, existence of a near-monopoly has created a temptation which few men can resist. This is the acceptance of as many as possible of the advertising dollars which sponsors literally beg to spend on broadcasting. There has been and there is a tendency of station ownership and management to expand the hours of sponsorship just because it is the easiest course to take.

Occasionally the temptation to take more money leads to the sale of the station at a price determined by the station's earning power rather than by the size of the investment which the first owner has made. For example, the $12 million paid in the illustration above was justified in terms of the earning power of the station. The new owner is thus required to continue earlier practices to protect his investment, even though in so doing he may provide a distinctly inferior program service.

The specific way in which the urge or need to make more money works to the disadvantage of the viewer is in the substitution of local or national spot sponsored programs in place of the sustaining public affairs programs provided by the networks. Each of the national networks assumes the responsibility of providing public affairs programs to its affiliates and over the years those broadcasts have been the high peaks of the American system. Unfortunately, many viewers never have a chance to see them. The major sponsored variety or western program on a network will be carried by a hundred and fifty or two hundred stations. The sustaining program which is carried by fifty outlets is considered an outstanding success.

Paradoxical as it seems, the local fare in many communities would be improved if there were fewer advertisers bidding for the time when network sustaining programs are available or if there were more stations to split up the advertising revenue.

The Future of Broadcasting

In spite of temporary handicaps the future of broadcasting appears to be extremely bright.

The number of television stations seems to be stalled at around 500 and no one at the moment has a solution to the economic problems of the ultra high frequencies which have caused the failure of some stations at the very moment others were making unbelievable profits.

In the summer of 1952, after a four-year moratorium on the consideration of license applications, the Federal Communications Commis-

[42]

sion resumed acceptance of new proposals. At that time a blueprint for the future was released which provided for approximately 2,000 stations in major and smaller communities and in the very high and ultra high frequencies. For a couple years there was the anticipated spurt in the numbers of both types of stations until it became clear that a UHF station could not survive with VHF competition. Since that time the number of UHF outlets has actually shrunk and no one seems now to have a solution to the problem.

However, when a member of the Federal Communications Commission visited the Syracuse University Campus in 1956, he expressed confidence that some day would see the change which would permit a nationwide system of more than 2,000 stations. Anyone who has watched past breakthroughs in radio must have a similar degree of confidence in American ingenuity.

At the end of the war in 1945 there were less than 1,000 AM radio stations on the air. A decade later the number approached 3,000 and is now headed far higher. Without doubt a similar growth can be anticipated in television.

Just as radio receivers have through the years become smaller, lighter, less expensive, and more portable, so should one expect that television sets of the future will be much more convenient. Manufacturers already predict that in the near future receivers will be purchased which look just like the picture which is hung on the wall. It will be compact and lightweight and easily purchased.

With the advent of better sets, one may also anticipate that television saturation of homes will become nearly as close to totality as is the current saturation of homes by radio. Only a decade ago scholars looked forward to television as a "quality medium" because the receivers were so expensive that only a few could afford them. Because of the close correlation between earning power and education, it was predicted that television would be used primarily by those who wanted to be challenged mentally in the evening.

However, the papers soon carried advertisements for sets which cost two dollars down and two dollars a week. Shortly, the lower income levels dominated the television audience and if there is any significant lag in a segment of our population, it is among the better educated who feel it is fashionable not to succumb to a medium with every appearance of mediocrity.

Just as radio can now transmit signals around the world, there is great promise that most of those who read these words will live to see television programs coming into their homes from all the continents. Whether they will show more interest in international television than they now show in international radio is a moot question, but the potential for world peace is most exciting.

There is no question but that radio and television will become more entertaining as the years pass and that they will occupy more time of Americans. There have always been those who said that broadcasting was a fad and people would soon tire of it and return to spending most of their time with books, magazine, newspapers, and movies. However, each week the Sindlinger Reports show just the opposite to be true. For example, for the week of April 13-19, 1958 the following report was made:

There were 124,782,000 people in the United States over 12 years of age. This is how they spent their time:

87,098,000 spent 1,725 million hours watching television each day
74,495,000 spent 1,011 million hours listening to radio each day
104,318,000 spent 405 million hours reading newspapers each day
42,551,000 spent 188 million hours reading magazines each day
24,910,000 spent 242 million hours watching movies on TV each day
30,426,000 spent 121 million hours attending movies during the week

The history of broadcasting indicates that both radio and television will consume more time of more Americans in the years to come.

As more people spend more time attending broadcasting than any other single activity with the exception of working and sleeping, the business world will continue to support the media prodigiously. If, in 1945, one could have predicted that the number of radio stations would rise from less than 1,000 to well over 3,000, most owners would gladly have sold their operations. Yet, at this time most stations are making more profits than ever and some operators will jokingly admit that it takes serious effort to operate a station at a loss. As long as the American economy stays reasonably healthy, an ever increasing number of stations can be expected to survive and flourish.

The Future of Broadcast Journalism

It is only in the context of consequence that the future of broadcasting looks dim. The past history of radio and television has been consistently weak in its lack of contribution to meeting the challenge posed at the outset of this chapter. More recently, broadcasting's reaction to the providential coincidence of possession of nuclear energy and the key to universal understanding has been to ignore the existence of both.

It should be quickly emphasized that the national networks have made a sincere attempt to program in the public interest. In some instances they have been most successful in communicating vital information to the people. When they have failed, it has frequently been because, as has been earlier demonstrated, the local affiliates disregarded the opportunity to carry significant material.

The weakness of broadcasting in meeting the challenge of our time can perhaps be traced to two factors: First, the challenge is not so obvious that it must be recognized. Indeed, some would question its existence. Second, the nature of television station ownership is significantly different from radio ownership of a few years ago. Many radio operators were truly interested in communicating and started their stations on a shoestring for that very purpose. These were the men who established such a brilliant record during the war years alluded to above.

The high original cost prevents the man who is interested in communication from entering the field of television. The corporate owner is now the rule and quite frequently the owner is an absentee from the community. In some instances the only contact between management and owner is the submission and perusal of the balance sheet. On occasion one finds that the absentee corporate owner is truly interested in the improvement of the community in which its station operates, but that interest has not been communicated to the management on the scene.

The chief attribute of the colonial newspaper and pamphlet was the intense interest of the individual publisher in the communication of his message. The increased significance of broadcasting as a medium will depend upon its ability to develop a tradition and devotion similar to that of the press. At the moment there are few indications that such development is in the offing.

In defining broadcasting's challenge it was suggested that the media should be used in five ways to help Americans solve their problems. When considered individually and specifically, the results are as follows:

First was the day-to-day coverage of daily events. Here the limiting factor is the amount of time devoted to it. From the networks come fifteen-minute summaries and from the stations neat five-minute packages which actually amount to four minutes and thirty seconds with time out for commercials. Network news time has been cut back in recent years and there is no indication that individual stations are increasing their newscasts to fill the gap. Too frequently, the criterion for item selection seems to be the amount and quality of the visual materials to accompany the script. Disproportionate amounts of time are given to those stories which occurred within view of a camera while far more significant items are covered in single sentences.

One seems justified in comparing news coverage by broadcasting with that available from the tabloid newspapers—enough to make persons think they are keeping up with the world but not enough to be important in influencing daily participation in its affairs.

Second is on-the-spot coverage of significant events. Although this is the area where television and radio have the greatest potential, many stations make no attempt at such service while the networks have done so well that it whets the appetite for more. Ratings show that a national political convention or the Army-McCarthy or Kefauver Committee hearings draw a healthy audience. However, they also cost a great deal of money and the viewer sees less and less of them as there is an opportunity to sell a regular schedule to an advertiser. A case in point is the rather intensive coverage of the United Nations in the late 1940's while there was no network coverage whatever of the sessions devoted to the Hungarian revolution in the fall of 1956.

The third area is in the feature programs which analyze in depth current problems. Frequently, these are documentaries which are of great interest and which can have great significance in our society. Here, again, the networks have done such outstanding work that one can only wish there were more. The *Project 20* series from the National Broadcasting Company and *See It Now* by the Columbia Broadcasting System are outstanding examples of what can be done. Other programs which concentrate on exposition of recent history such as *The Twentieth Century* and *Victory At Sea* are equally illustrious.

The programs cited have been extremely successful because they were sponsored and, therefore, carried by a full complement of affiliates. Unfortunately, most stations do not attempt such programming and the networks are unable to secure the number of sponsors they need to expand their efforts.

There is little that can be said about the presentation of controversial issues by discussion except that it just isn't done very much. Again, the networks have presented some programs of great excellence but the stations have done little.

The chief criticism to be leveled against each of the program areas above is that there is no organized effort to present a well rounded schedule which attempts to meet each of the needs of modern man.

Finally, and perhaps most important, is the area of leadership of public opinion. A basis for the philosophy of Freedom of Speech is that if people in a democracy have an opportunity to hear enough ideas, they will then be able to make intelligent decisions at the polls and elsewhere in citizen participation. It is in this area of leadership or editorializing that the press has traditionally done its finest work.

Nearly two decades ago the Federal Communications Commission ruled in the Mayflower Decision that a station could not be an advocate. It reasoned that radio facilities were limited and an opposition could not start a new station to present the other side. Therefore, no station would be permitted to take sides in politics or other controversial issues.

For several years the broadcasters fought the Commission ruling with every strength at their command. They cited the First Amendment to the Constitution and accused the Commission of being un-American and opposed to the operation of the democratic process.

Finally, the Commission did amend its ruling: henceforth broadcasters were permitted to editorialize provided they made equal time available to a responsible person from the opposition. In the subsequent decade the right to editorialize has been used less and less. Today when a station does take a strong position, it is hailed by the trade press as a news item of first magnitude.

In short, while the broadcaster clamors for his right to express an opinion, he has shown little evidence of believing in anything strongly enough to be willing to give up commercial time in order to express himself.

It is at this point that the most important characteristic of broadcasting becomes evident. Most people in the business consider themselves part of the entertainment world with a primary function of attracting to the receivers enough audience so that the advertiser will be glad to sponsor the time and pay the bills.

There have been enough excellent examples of broadcast journalism to make one confident that man does indeed now hold in one hand the key to universal understanding. Until the broadcaster looks upon himself as more than an entertainer, it is difficult to see how we can expect more than entertainment from these marvels of communication which have been bestowed upon us.

V

Magazines

ROLAND E. WOLSELEY

MR. JOHN B. W. BROWN, manager of the Center City, New York, office of the Major Life Insurance Company, walked into his living room after eating his dinner, one day in December, A.D. 2000.

"Think I'll do a little reading," he said, half aloud, and proceeded to choose a magazine. He arose, went to the viewing room down the hall. He had only a short time before furnished the room. He relished it, equipped as it was like a small theater. Last night he had had a dozen people in to use the small and simple machines to read newspapers, books, and magazines; to look at photographs, slides, and instant blow-ups of clippings; to see a full-length movie and television show, both in color.

Mr. Brown slid open a door on a cabinet about 10 inches wide, 5 inches high, and 8 inches deep. He revolved a dial, then hesitated a few moments while making up his mind. He could have the current issues of *Coropage, Readshort, Cosmopost, Lookalife,* and a dozen other popular magazines. Finally he stopped the dial at No. 8, *Readshort,* pressed a red button, and watched as a green light pulsed beside the dial for a minute. A click announced that his magazine had arrived. A sheaf of film, 3 by 5 inches, gradually issued from a slot at the bottom of the machine. He put this into the magazine viewer and settled back in a chair.

The viewer enlarged the magazine page to 40 inches by 40 inches; it was changed back and forth to other pages simply by pressing a remote control button. When he had finished, Mr. Brown slipped the little film packet into a box marked *Readshort,* in the proper monthly slot. As he did so he remembered how, when he was a boy, his father had tried to save all issues of *Lookalife,* in the days when it was printed on big sheets of paper. A tower of magazines had dominated one side of the basement.

Something he had seen in this issue of *Readshort* reminded him of an article he had read at the office in a magazine called *The Insurance Executive.* He had brought the film home; he slightly opened his air-conditioned suit to get at it. He decided to slip this into the automatic reader also. He read for a half hour more.

A piece of science fiction about journalism? Possibly, but as science fiction came into greater plausibility at mid-century, as Jules Verne's and H. G. Wells's imaginations took on startling reality, it is unwise to assume that the above scene in the first decade of the twenty-first century is necessarily nonsense. Its author does not expect to live to verify it, although he hopes that science soon will discover ways to keep the body and mind normally alive for many years beyond the usual seventy so that he can be here to see what magazines really will be like about A.D. 2010.

At any rate, magazines will be different by then because so many of the conditions for using them will have changed.

If ordinary citizens by that time will be riding in wheelless automobiles at 500 miles an hour or in spaceships traveling at the speed of light, as predicted by engineers and scientists now, magazines will have to adjust to the new behavior of their readers and advertisers.

Not only will readers be flashing over and along the earth's surface at what may at mid-century seem impossible speeds, but the development engineers also see other changes that will affect magazines.

By 2000 it is possible that waste water from paper production will be a common source of food. The oceans and seas as well as the land will be mined in search of isotopes that will provide atomic energy, and will be farmed for food not known today. H. J. Rand, president of the development corporation bearing his name, forecasts that "the sea will be turned into hundreds of valuable chemicals, as the air now is. New fibers, new finishes, new materials of all kinds will come from the laboratories, affecting everything we eat, wear, and use." Greater energy, provided by nuclear fuels, such as uranium or heavy hydrogen, can hardly skip the magazine business in bringing its benefits to printing and other operations.

Automation seems destined to click and thump its way into magazine journalism even more than it has already. The first signs of terrifying invasion of the editorial rooms came as this was being written. The International Business Machines Corporation announced the "Auto-Abstract," an electronic machine "that will read a magazine article and then write an abstract of it."

When a certain widely known magazine editor read about this in a New York newspaper he did not finish the article, he told the author of this chapter.

"Why not?" he was asked.

"I couldn't do it. It gave me an inferiority complex. They'll develop this thing so that editors won't be needed any more," he said.

[50]

He may not be far wrong. The device can condense lengthy reports. Other machines already in use can read addressed envelopes and sort them. Automatic indexing is already being done at high speeds.

If, as also forecast, unmanned freight rockets will transport mail from one coast of the United States to the other in an hour, the production schedules of magazines will be affected profoundly. Dr. Wernher von Braun, the rocket expert, has predicted that within a hundred years the earth will be surrounded by artificial satellites, some of which will receive messages "radioed up to them while over one city, country or continent, and play them back while over another." He also said that a few communications satellites would handle the entire volume of private and official communications between all points of the earth more than 500 miles apart. Other satellites would serve as television stations.

As a result of these development a magazine which so desired could cover events as speedily as could newspapers, bringing these two media even closer together than is being done at present by the rapid sending of copy and setting of type by newsmagazines and newsletters.

To retain distinctiveness, magazines then would have to offer content that is increasingly analytical and interpretive. But they would benefit from the new transmission speeds in the gathering of information and pictures. Possibly through an adaptation of facsimile, magazines of great physical beauty could be produced quickly in the subscriber's home. Or, as Mr. Brown lived to see, everything will be on film.

All such developments depend, of course, upon their cost to the publisher. It already is possible to perform numerous scientific miracles, but they are uneconomical. If any of the predictions made in this chapter do not materialize the reason may well be traced to the inability of economists to keep pace with scientists.

"The intellectual output of the brain should be greatly increased," in the opinion of Dr. John Weir, of the California Institute of Technology faculty. He foresees much more efficient educational techniques than now used. These presumably would enable the magazine reader to appreciate and comprehend far more weighty content than he now will accept. Thus the egghead magazines—the journals of scholarship, the serious weeklies and monthlies of ideas and opinions—may well become common rather than little known, as today. What will replace them? More experimental periodicals, perhaps, such as the present obscure "little" magazines. Through their experiments with ideas and artistic forms, these magazines may achieve a prominence far beyond the dreams of their editors.

At any rate, no one who has expressed himself publicly doubts that magazines do have a future, although there is no agreement on what that future will look like. Ben Hibbs, editor of *The Saturday Evening Post,* speaking before the Public Relations Society of America in 1957, expressed the common view of the industry's leaders when he said:

> Sometimes we magazine people are asked whether our business has a future. I'd like to answer that question with an emphatic, "Yes." Despite all the new forms of competition that have been thrown at us, aggregate magazine circulations today are growing faster than the population of this country—always a healthy sign. During the past ten years television has swept across the nation like a prairie fire, yet during this same period readership figures on the content of magazines have remained fairly constant. If you don't believe that people are reading magazines, all you have to do is to sit where I sit, publish something controversial, something that stirs people up, and then watch the mailbags full of letters come in—and duck the brickbats.
>
> Moreover, I firmly believe that despite all the new diversions, despite all the demands on people's time, there will always be a large segment of our population which wants something informative and entertaining to read. And so long as people do want something to read, there will be a continuing place in their lives for the magazines— provided the magazines are intelligently edited.

Mr. Hibbs gave no indication of how far into the future he was looking. But Dr. Frank Luther Mott, the noted historian of American magazines and newspapers, writing in 1954 and looking ahead "a decade or two," also had no doubt that magazines would continue, although his prognostications varied by types.

Much too soon it is, of course, to test Dean Mott's forecasts, but they are revealing when examined even only five years later. He declared that "the next decade or two will see the obliteration of the distinction between the general literary monthly and the low-priced book in its laminated cover. I think the general literary monthly is doomed; that it is actually obsolescent at this time."

So far he has been partly right on this point. He was referring no doubt to *Harper's* and *The Atlantic*. Both have given more and more space to nonliterary subjects. *The Saturday Review* and *The Reporter* have joined them and they too have great interest in business, science, politics, and other such topics.

But his expectations for the low-priced book devoted to "original and varied content" have not yet been realized. The few so far attempted either have died or have been reduced to annual or semiannual frequency: *Discovery, The Seven Arts,* and *Pocket Book* have disappeared; *The Anchor Review* and *Modern Writing* come out irregularly; only *New World Writing* is dependable and *The Evergreen Review* is at this writing too new to have been tested.

But what kinds of magazines are we all writing about? It should be understood that Mr. Hibbs had in mind consumer magazines, whereas it is our duty in this chapter to consider the future of all types of periodicals, specialized as well as consumer. The two general groups of magazines are newsstand magazines for general circulation, and periodicals dealing with religion, science, sports, education, and scores of other specialized subjects.

To get perspective on the predictions made in this chapter we should have a quick overview of the magazine world as it looks at this writing. In the United States there are about 12,500 magazines. This number is more than half of all the journalistic publications issued. About 300 are consumer or general, 2,000 are business (often called trade), 8,500 industrial (house organs of various types), 1,500 are religious, and the rest deal with other specialties. Circulations and advertising revenue in the aggregate are at their highest. This country publishes the most widely circulated and read magazine in the world (*The Reader's Digest*, with an international circulation of 20 million and a readership of 85 million) as well as the largest number of different magazines. More than 60 have circulations of one million or higher.

What the future holds for this giant industry will, of course, differ for the individual magazine and the groups as well. A company employee magazine with 3,000 free circulation a month that does not sell space for advertising will be much less affected than a huge newsstand publication of five million paid circulation a week.

Predictions about any medium in mass communications might well be divided into short- and long-range forecasts. Because of the directions in which the magazine world now is moving it might be well to divide the portents into a ten-year short-range group and a fifty-year long-range group, examining the magazines by standard departments. All these predictions, whatever the range, are made on the assumption that there will not be a severe world depression or catastrophic war or the accession of a dictatorship government.

Short-Range Predictions

Advertising: The expenditures on advertising in all magazines selling space have grown in the past decade by $300 million. Considering the rate at which new products and services are being produced, this growth rate will be continued. The production cost per thousand copies, which rose for magazines as a whole between 1950 and 1957 (or nearly 30 per cent) will rise simultaneously with investment. Business magazines will show a marked increase in advertising volume. G. Carroll Buzby, president of the Chilton Company, a firm issuing a group of such periodicals, and one of the most astute of the business publishers, predicted late in 1957 that "Within a very few years it (the business magazine volume of advertising) will pass the half billion mark." He pointed out that the advertising volume for all business papers "is over six times what it was in 1940 and will probably total somewhere over $470 million in 1958." For many years the leaders in advertising volume (as distinct from advertising revenue) have been the business magazines. This condition will continue. Dollar returns will still be greater among consumer magazines, for they will have to raise their rates in order further to offset the staggeringly high production costs as circulations mount.

Circulation: On the short view, circulations will rise, because of population increases and the unwillingness of magazine operators to relax their highly complicated efforts to win it. The trend is toward increase. Consumer magazine circulations have jumped 37 per cent from 1947 to 1957, or almost double the population increase. Greater effort will be made to win newsstand acceptance, since this is now flabby and is the chief source of new subscribers. Methods of distribution will remain about the same; the newly formed wholesale distributing firms will increase in number and in size, but none will again reach the monopolistic position once held by the American News Company. Specialized magazine circulations will remain small, in general, although a few that will turn to controlled circulation on a mass distribution basis will achieve high distribution, especially in technical fields.

Editorial: The long campaign to make magazines easier to read will reach full fruition during the next decade. This result will come as much through more simplified writing as via typographical choices. The technological world, especially, has become so complex that readers must be given more signposts, more short cuts, more aids to absorb at least the nonfiction content of their periodicals. More and more magazines will experiment to meet the needs, both consumer and specialized.

Subject matter will continue to be dominantly factual rather than fictional. The problem of editing for a world, instead of a single nation, of readers will be accentuated, and will make for broader topics and more contributions from writers beyond our own national boundaries. Pictures will recede in importance, especially from consumer books, because of the technological advances in television and photography. The latter will be far cheaper and more commonly available.

If a person can carry with him a small box about the size of a midget radio on which he can pick up television images from all over the world he will rely less on pictures in his magazines. But during this decade there will be only a lessening of emphasis, as already typified by the inclusion of far more text than originally was intended in both *Look* and *Life*.

Management: Specialized magazines will be safer investments than those intended solely for the general consumer. Dean Mott wrote in 1954 that "class magazines will go on kaleidoscopically forever." The staff of *Printer's Ink,* at 1957's end, forecast that because "low publisher profits make magazine investment highly speculative" there will be fewer, but larger, magazines. They and others agree that this trend is explained by such increasing costs as those of material, labor, circulation, and "doing business" generally. This situation results in small, marginal operations being less and less attractive. Only the larger companies will be able to launch new consumer magazines and withstand the costs of the existing ones. More mergers will occur, as will more deaths of magazine giants.

All publishing companies, large or small, will in the next ten years re-examine costs in all departments. They began to do this early in 1958, moved by the recession. New thought will be given to cost controls. One of the areas to be examined most carefully will be production. From 1945 to 1957 the costs here rose astoundingly. Paper, for instance, increased in price 97 per cent between those years. There will be more reliance on co-operation between magazines through such organizations as the Magazine Publishers Association, its subsidiary, Magazine Advertising Bureau; Associated Business Publications, National Business Publications, as well as of publishers of more specialized periodicals. MPA already has made a beginning with its newly prepared materials on scientific cost-control and operational budgeting.

Profit margins will differ not only as between consumer and specialized magazines but also between magazines within either group. In publicly held publishing companies at least (figures not being available for the privately held firms), earnings have been dropping. To keep them up or bring them higher may depend on reducing costs, which in turn can be accomplished not only by more careful control of expenditures but also by consolidation of certain operations. One of these now increasingly common in the newspaper world is combining business but not other departments. The Birmingham (Ala.) *News* and the Birmingham *Post Herald,* for example, although each owned by a different company, co-operate on business operations in their city. This sort of unity is rare between magazines not commonly owned, only *Harper's* and *The Atlantic,* among periodicals of influence or importance, having done anything similar.

Another approach, not now widely employed either, will be to cut down costly circulation promotion. The most dramatic example is *The New Yorker,* which asserts it has "almost no circulation promotion expense." One of its vice presidents, E. R. Spaulding, was quoted by *Tide* as saying that "We don't try to buy readers." *Cosmopolitan* in its time has cut off subscription circulation, reduced its guarantee from two million to seven hundred thousand and cut advertising rates. In 1958 *Farm Journal* followed a similar policy. This stratagem is more feasible for the specialized magazine than the consumer, but will be engaged in more commonly as production costs mount.

No one knows, of course, what such technological changes as those mentioned at the outset of this chapter will do for cost savings. Other developments may be beneficial to magazines in paper, typesetting, engraving, printing, and even editing. Magazine management will be quick to avail itself of whatever inventions come forth, for it has been far more progressive than other printed media (newspapers and books) in developing and using the results of technological experiments, as witness the special plant maintained for this purpose by Time Inc., and the experimental work being done in their regular plants by other firms that print their own or other publications, such as Curtis, McCall's, and Meredith.

Other ways to offset mounting costs will be used: advertising, per copy, and subscription rates all will be raised; these figures already are higher and will continue to climb, although possibly not to the minimum of a dollar a copy for a monthly as recommended by Ralph Barton, editor of *Media/scope,* several years back. Unless cost reductions can be effected in other ways, higher income achieved in these fashions may be the only solution. And the efficacy of this policy by management depends, of course, on the state of the economy and the degree of disadvantage in which this would leave magazines. Pay-television might be a deciding factor here.

During the next ten years nothing significant will be accomplished to settle the ethical problem of the conflict between editorial and advertising content. At present every magazine's management is selling the reader's faith in the publication. This trust in the periodical is being sold to advertisers; unless they live up to that faith the magazine is bound to suffer. Among scores of consumer magazines the reader is being defrauded by publishers who sell space to manufacturers of worthless products, or if not worthless, announced as accomplishing something which they do not accomplish as promised. This unethical practice takes place mainly in the magazines that are published obviously to exploit public interest in sex, entertainment, and crime. Ethical self-control will be somewhat stricter, but nothing fundamental can be done because under today's economic burdens publishers of magazines, both ethical and unethical, cannot venture into cooperative or nonprofit publishing. Evidence of small changes that have taken place that point to slow but large ones are the alterations in *Confidential* and the public frownings upon the girly magazines which has led to a decrease among their number or a change in their emphasis.

Production: Costs will be watched especially carefully here. Consumer magazines will venture into more regional editions, a marked trend already noted in 1958, when *TV Guide* had forty-nine editions, most of them printed at widely separated points. Greater interest than ever before will be shown in production experiments, as for example "smoke" printing. Magazines are likely to be more often pocket size or 8 x 10 rather than 9 x 12, not only because picture display will decrease gradually from its present prominent place to a more moderate use (although never to the point of virtual nonuse as in many magazines of the late nineteenth century and early twentieth) but also because paper costs will be affected. Issues will be thinner because advertisers are not satisfied to have their displays, especially in consumer periodicals, lost among several hundreds of pages of colorful advertising. This change, however, will not come about markedly in the specialized magazines, even though the advertising volume there is great, because such advertising is more nearly what has been characterized as "newsvertising." Thinner magazines will make for reduced mailing expense and will cut costs all along the production line. Some magazines will be issued more frequently, rather than have pages eliminated; that is, monthlies will in some instances become biweeklies. Each issue will thus be less bulky but the advertising and editorial volume over a year's time will be maintained.

Research: In the fight to cut costs, research of all kinds in the magazine field will be increased. Typical of the work which will be done are the readership surveys that have been made through their own particular systems by McGraw-Hill (which calls it "reader feed-back"), Hayden (reader recall system), and Reinhold (Computer-Dex, which tries to determine action as well as attention). The various independent research firms will be busier than ever in digging to find facts not only about readership but also about reader interest, reader conduct or choices, and other areas for research, including legibility of types. All this will be in addition to technological research in production methods and equipment. Emphasis also will be placed on staff analysis, especially through the personnel department.

Long-Range Predictions

Much of what is predicted for the short-range period will, of course, overlap with the years from 1970 on. This section will present a brief forecast, however, of what magazines will be like by the first decade of the next century, assuming that the bulk of the short-range forecasts have materialized and probably been accepted and even accentuated.

Beginning with the lifeblood of journalism—advertising—it is clear that despite American population rises (600,000,000 by 2000 is the present forecast) and the possibilities of greater circulation revenue, magazines still will depend heavily on advertising revenue, regardless of whether they are produced on film, paper, aluminum, or some other substance. Communities will be smaller and cities will be used less and less for residences and will be almost totally working areas, but goods and services will still have to be announced and promoted. With more people, and more of them then ever before young, the advertising appeal will be angled strongly at the young and middle-aged.

More rapid and commodious transportation will have two effects upon the next important area, that of circulation: it will cut down use of magazines on transportation but at the same time make international and national distribution easier. Circulation may by the end of this century be much more under control than it is today. Some will be free and some paid, and both will be considered respectable and effective. Long ago it seemed not altogether desirable to have a lot of it. Ben Hibbs, in his speech to the Public Relations Society, also said that one of the problems of magazines then was what he called "the current rat-race for larger and larger circulations." He cautioned editors not to become "so bemused by the numbers game that they forget their responsibilities." Methods of reading, such as Mr. Brown's viewing machine, will expand the readership of magazines but not necessarily enlarge their circulation. Such machines could be used in schools, for instance, and expose hundreds of students to magazine pages they might not otherwise see. If circulation and its promotion become too expensive magazines will set arbitrary limits to their distribution, yet not interfere with their educational importance.

International distribution not only will be easier but the greater unity of the world also will encourage more foreign language editions of magazines from various countries (as, for example, technical magazines already being published in several languages between the same covers). Stepped-up trade—both imports and exports—will make it necessary for advertising agencies to have more foreign affiliations and thus they will be in a better position to service advertising departments of magazines. This wider distribution also will broaden the scope and influence of house, business, technical, and the more general and simply edited consumer magazine.

Specialized magazines will increase the depth of their news and editorial content and also be more numerous. When interplanetary travel is as commonplace as air navigation of the globe is today, magazines will have to serve all the new technical areas with news and interpretation of events. Just as we now have magazines for various subdivisions of surface transportation (*Model Railroader* and *Railway Locomotives and Cars,* for example) so space travel will require its own periodical content. Certainly if human life is discovered on other planets it will move enterprising publishers on this one to transport magazines to serve such folk, once the language barrier is overcome, even if the residents of Mars, or whatever it may be, have their own periodicals. Writers and artists will be drawn from all over the world and perhaps even outside it or from within it. Editing and other office operations will likely be largely mechanized; possibly the only reminder of the use of human judgment will come in the final selection of copy and the determination of policy.

Since there doubtless will be more women in the various occupations and more work done at home by both men and women because of the break-up of the cities forecast by some sociologists, management will see to it that more technical and other specialized magazines will be provided. General women's magazines, like men's, will have disappeared in favor of family periodicals. Management will have to provide, along with subscriptions, tape recordings of parts of the content for learning during sleep. Group publishing will be more common than ever, because more economical and efficient in both the consumer and the specialized areas. Organizations, specifically the Associated Business Publications and the National Business Publications, will have merged by this century's end. Management will by then have to sign labor union contracts with coverage of all departments, instead of only with printers, engravers, and other craft groups. A new union will spring up and organize all employees of magazine companies except those of impecunious publishers of extremely advance guard experimental magazines. This union will be dominantly on the editorial side.

The propagandistic periodicals, which are a large section of the specialized magazines, have a diverse future. The magazines that serve labor and management will continue to exist at opposite poles so long as these entities remain unmerged. There is no sign of their complete integration, although they have drawn together in the past quarter of a century until now both labor and management can be called big business. All that has happened is that they have the same profiles but they are still antagonistic. This means that house organs and labor magazines will have a function, even though they may conform to the physical changes generally expected.

The political magazine, at best a shadow in the United States when compared with such periodicals in other Western nations, will flourish for the first time since Revolutionary War days if the country continues to move toward top-heavy government and eventually some sort of Americanized totalitarianism. It then will be a thoroughly doctrinaire magazine.

The magazines for social minorities—for the Negro people and for the foreign language groups, particularly—are likely to disappear completely, several types of integration having weakened these propaganda presses for more than a decade already. By A.D. 2000 the United States, as Edwin Embree forecast many years ago, will be without its people of black skin, and what now is brown America will be even lighter in shade. Replacing the foreign language press will be one printed in Esperanto or some other international language; more likely there will be no publications of any sort in the United States in any language except the American.

Magazines on film and magazines that will read themselves will be characteristic. The first of these production miracles will have various forms, depending upon their function. The second will be films with sound-track so that a "reader" will see the page on the screen which would be too great to permit reading and have it read to him simultaneously. Many of the preliminary operations used today, such as typesetting, engraving, and printing from type or plates will have fallen into disuse as photography replaces such operations. All this will reduce the bulk and awkwardness of present-day production, permit faster production, and easy transport and storage of results. Automation will be in full swing in the production world.

Promotion will fall into considerable disuse in the circulation realm but continue to be needed in advertising. Already it is costly to promote circulation; it would be even more so when circulation has more nearly reached the saturation point under the new methods of distribution and reading. It will be used more by trade organizations for the benefit of the magazine industry as a whole: to sell the virtues of magazine advertising, of the magazine as an educational tool, and as a rewarding place to be employed.

Having passed its peak with the successful blanketing of the world with the new types of almost automatic magazines, research will continue largely as a recorder of history, as a source of information about the success of the various new devices used in producing magazines, and for experimentation within the areas still costly to magazine management.

"The future," Ben Hibbs once said, "is only a projection of the present." It is not to be expected, then, that every reader will agree even with a small portion of this forecast. He is always free to make his own projection, based on his own knowledge of what constitute the present and its potentialities. It seems evident, however, that if magazines do not seek to adjust to the new times to come that they will disappear, despite the confidence of their present leaders.

VI

Advertising

PHILIP WARD BURTON

ALTHOUGH ADVERTISING CAN TRACE its origins back to the Egyptians, almost no one in advertising—in the working advertising world, that is—looks back ten years, let alone to the days of the Pharaohs. Because of the constant pressures of advertising, most of its practitioners function on a day-to-day basis. There is little interest in the past, and few have time to speculate on any future that extends beyond five or ten years. The working advertising man finds that the details of fashioning next year's campaign usually give him all the future he can handle. Prognostications as to what might happen five to fifty years from the present are usually left to the upper echelon of advertising, a group that has the time to contemplate what the years may bring.

Peering into the future is, however, becoming more and more important to the planners of advertising. Much of this "peering" can only be guesswork. How many, for example, who were crystal-gazing in the thirties could have envisioned the complete demise of network radio? Despite such uncertainties, advertising has become too vital a force to be entrusted entirely to the day-to-day, year-to-year planners. Advertising is inextricably tied to people, to population, to the great changes that are occurring in America. What is going to happen to the population in the coming years is going to affect advertising profoundly. Advertising must be ready for these changes if it is to attain full efficiency.

What are these consumer changes that will affect advertising? Certainly, one of the most important is the aging of our population. Growth of households will be determined by persons at the extremes of the age scale, those under 30 and those more than 50. Growth for these two groups will exceed the growth for those in the middle group. These tendencies are indicated in the following table.[1]

[1] "Advertising's Enigma, The Changing Consumer," *Tide*, March 14, 1958, p. 22.

Age of household heads in the United States

Age	1956 (millions)	(%)	1965 (millions)	(%)
Under 30	6.4	13.0	7.8	13.9
30-39	12.0	24.5	11.9	21.3
40-49	10.3	20.9	11.6	20.6
50-64	12.7	25.8	15.2	27.2
65 and more	7.8	15.8	9.5	17.0

Up to this point advertising men have not agreed about the worth of the older market. Some have tended to build dreams about the market potentiality in this group. These dreams are built on the fact that the net worth of this group is higher than that of any group except the 55-64 group. Yet, millions in the older group will exist principally on social security income, not exactly a promising market for the advertiser. This group will be inviting to drug manufacturers, but daunting to sellers of products for outdoor recreation. Products of comfort and convenience will find acceptance among older persons but clothing items such as suits and slacks will find a poor market.

Despite some of the weaknesses of this group as an advertising market it will need to be cultivated because it will be a big market and its members will have money to spend. Advertisers, consequently, will need to shape their creative approach to fit the preferences of those members. Copy should be toned down to a more conservative pitch. Radio and television programming will have a different character.

Another significant change in the character of the population will be the continued increase in the white collar group—professional men, proprietors, managers, clerical workers, and salesmen. This group will increase more rapidly than the blue collar group and will contrast even more sharply with the farm group that will decline steadily. Along with the increase of the white collar group will be a steady lessening of the onetime sharp sociological differences between white collar workers and those in the skilled and semiskilled blue collar class. Advertisers must assume that the huge portion of the total market composed by these workers—white collar and blue collar—will be more discriminating and, at the same time, more uniform in its tastes. Without *being* white collar workers, for example, there will be millions in the blue collar group who will have the same status symbols as the white collar group.

Some idea of the changing employment picture that is causing such deep changes in our national life, and in our marketing approach is given in the following table.[2]

2 "Advertising's Enigma, The Changing Consumer," *Tide*, March 14, 1958, p. 22.

Trends in occupation groups in the United States

	Past	Present		Projected
	1910	1955	1956	1965
Total	100.0%	100.0%	100.0%	100.0%
White collar	*22.3*	*38.7*	*39.8*	*41.6*
Professional	4.6	9.2	9.5	10.6
Proprietors, managers	7.3	9.8	9.8	9.9
Clerical and sales	10.4	19.7	20.5	21.1
Blue collar	*37.4*	*40.2*	*38.9*	*40.3*
Skilled	11.8	13.4	13.3	14.0
Semiskilled	14.1	20.8	20.1	21.3
Unskilled	11.5	6.0	5.5	5.0
Service	9.6	*11.3*	*11.6*	*11.1*
Farmers and Farm workers	*30.7*	*9.8*	*9.8*	*7.0*

Consider the realignments of the consumer markets in accordance with the shifting age groups and occupational groups. Then, add to these changes still more changes resulting from the fact that a higher and higher percentage of the citizens will be given high school and college diplomas. Add to this development the steady increase in leisure hours for Americans. All of these factors carry strong implications for advertisers—in the kind of products they market, and in the way they fashion their creative approach. Of these factors, education is the key. An educated market is a better spending market and this *will* be a better educated market with a tripling and ultimately quadrupling of the number of those presently attending college.

Estimates have indicated that the households, the heads of which have had some college background, spend on the average almost twice as much as those households headed by those who have not gone beyond high school. While the better educated audience may present a greater creative challenge to the advertiser it will, at the same time, be a more responsive audience once the right tone and selling appeals have been established.

A fascinating field for conjecture is what will happen to the different forms of advertising—consumer, business, farm, government. There will be changes but it does not look as if the changes will be revolutionary. It is to be doubted that the changes will be so pronounced as between the 1920's and the 1950's, for example. In this period, the most noticeable differences were in the quality of mechanical production, the writing of copy claims that could stand some sort of legal inspection, and the general writing quality of the advertisements—along with the improvement in advertising art-work and photography. Changes in the years ahead will be in these same areas but it is doubtful that they will be so striking as in the past thirty years.

Consumer advertising will become more believable. The artificial dialogue in print and in sound will be replaced by conversation that sounds like natural conversation between two real human beings instead of a carefully manufactured promotional "spiel" delivered by two models who have no connection with real-life people.

Consumer audiences, already restive, will finally laugh out of existence the kind of absurd situation commercials found today in radio and television —the type in which one of the characters acts as a "stooge" for another character and feeds copy openings which are seized upon eagerly by the second person who thereby launches into long declamations about the product.

Today, there are two types of language. There is the natural language that can be heard between people in subways, on street corners, in homes, in hotel lobbies, and in business offices. Then there is the language of advertising that is found *only* in advertising. This language, full of extravagances, pomposities, and artificialities, is so markedly different from the natural language referred to, that the general public has come more and more to dismiss it as "advertising talk." Such a term applied to advertising copy carries an implication that in the copy there is a certain glibness, slickness, and overtone of dishonesty. This *is* the opinion of the consumer today of advertising copy.

One of advertising's biggest challenges of the future is to change this opinion and this will be done, *must* be done if advertising is to have stature and power as a selling force.

Consumer advertisers will emphasize even more than they do today the image-building approach. There will be more and more standardization of products, and there will be more and more products. In the welter of products and copy points for the products, consumers will find, even more than today, a difficulty in remembering which advertiser is saying what things about his product. Image-building will, accordingly, become important. Advertisers will create identification for their products and their product messages by creating a favorable image for the company advertising those products. General Motors, General Electric, Du Pont, and Squibb have long used advertising to create a corporate image. They will continue to do so in the future and many others not now employing this technique will do so, too.

Even in straight product advertising, consumer advertisers will do less importuning of the audience than they do today. The better educated, more sophisticated consumer of the future will resent even more than he does today the pitchman approach. Gradually, hard-sell will vanish; the soft-sell that takes its place will be more intelligently conceived, more persuasive in the long run than today's hard-sell and will be far more bearable to the more sensitive audience of the future than the jarring clamor produced by today's hard-sell advertisers.

Because the consumer audience of the future will be more analytical in its buying, the advertising directed to this audience will resort less to emotional appeals. Replacing the say-nothing, frothy approach in much of today's advertising will be copy that gives reasons for buying. The consumer will be able, better than he is today, to make a buying decision from the advertising.

Aiding the consumer—and the honest advertiser, too—will be a greatly strengthened Federal Trade Commission. Instead of hamstringing this department by denying it adequate operating funds, the government will give it ample money and personnel. Today, the Federal Trade Commission, our most important means of external safeguarding of advertising honesty, is made weak because the government's niggardly budgets force the commission to operate with a skeleton working force. This has enabled many advertisers to attempt advertising they would not use if they knew that the Federal Trade Commission were fully staffed. As it is, the Commission does not have an adequate force to ferret out advertising that is dishonest, or if it finds such advertising, to try guilty advertisers quickly. Cases before the Commission may be held over for months, or years, because of the personnel lack. The government cannot continue to ignore this safeguarding of the consumers' interests and ultimately will provide the people with a fully staffed Federal Trade Commission. Advertisers, the bulk of whom are honest, will welcome the chastising of those relatively few dishonest advertisers whose actions have always discredited all advertising men.

Business advertising will probably see less change than consumer advertising. Almost all of it will continue to be found in publications, as it is today. Creatively, it will be executed largely as it is now, with some changes, however, that will differentiate it from today's business advertising. Although today's factual business publication advertisements will be used, there will be much more use of corporate advertising to go along with factual advertising. Image-building advertising will increase in business publications, as it will in consumer publications. Advertisers will stress their corporate personalities. They will almost be driven to this means of identity-establishing as business publications become even more numerous and as the individual issues become thicker and thicker with advertisements.

Today's trend toward greater care in the writing of business publication copy will result eventually in the consistent use of the finest creative talent in the fashioning of business advertising. There will be little tendency to do what has been done so often—to assign the poorest writers to business advertising. Such advertising will have achieved full stature; it will be executed with the same care given to expensive consumer campaigns.

Farm advertising, like business advertising, should not change radically but it will experience some changes nonetheless. Creative approaches will reflect the changing character of the farm market. A greater sophistication in the writing will constitute a recognition of a farm market that is better educated than today—that has money for education, and refinements in everyday living. In accordance with the national trend in business, farms are getting bigger today; the trend will continue. Marginal farmers, scratching out a miserable existence, will give way to the big-business farmer who applies scientific farming methods on his hundreds or thousands of acres. The new farmer will be a student of marketing and cost accounting; just as much as possible he will reduce the hazards that have traditionally made agriculture a fearsome occupation.

Our new farmer—trained in scientific agriculture and latest business methods—cannot be approached as if he were some straw-chewing rustic. Even today it is risky to employ creative approaches in farm advertising that imply in the slightest way that the farm reader or listener has anything of the "rube" about him. In the future, such an implication will be disastrous if used in advertising for the new breed of farmer.

Today's farm advertising offers much proof to substantiate product claims. Tomorrow's farm advertising will be even more heavily laden with proof—from agricultural schools, from government sources, from county agents. While weather, changing markets and commodity prices, and fluctuating economic cycles will always inject a certain amount of uncertainty into farming, the future farmer's efforts will be wholly devoted to cutting down the amount of that uncertainty; he will do little bowing of his head, accepting agricultural troubles as a manifestation of divine will. Instead, he will look in all directions to find ways out of his difficulties. If he can find help in advertising, he will utilize advertising but he will be savage in condemnation of advertising that offers no real help, that fails to back up claims, or that in any way twists the facts. This farmer of the future will be a new hard-boiled breed; woe to the farm advertiser who fails to measure up to the demands of the changing agriculturist.

Another field for advertising that will develop over the years will be government advertising. Such growth is inevitable as "big government," with us since the 1930's, gets bigger all the time. Big government is pervasive, reaching into all fields, in all directions, entering into all lives. To attain its objectives it must use all forms of communication and propaganda. That big government would find increasingly useful one of the most powerful of communication instruments—advertising—is no surprise. Government on all levels—municipal, county, state, and national—has utilized advertising; it seems safe to say that today's use of advertising by government will be viewed as modest by the government men of the future. Today, government employs advertising to get out the vote, to promote bond issues, to make understandable (or palatable) government directives, to recruit for the armed services.

Big government of the future will be a gigantic advertiser. Perhaps, however, it is unfair to advertising to use the term "advertising" to describe the government's use of the medium. A better description: that the government will apply advertising techniques to propaganda activities. Thus, big government of the future will advertise intensively: (1) to inform the public about latest government directives and activities; (2) to propagandize in order to create a favorable public opinion toward objectives sought by government leaders. While the use of the word "propagandize" might seem to imply a slightly shameful use of advertising it may be said that the use of advertising for propaganda purposes is far less insidious than many other means that can be used. A government advertisement is an open declaration compared to a government handout that burrows its way into editorial material of newspapers and magazines.

If one were to point to one development as the most striking that has taken place in the last twenty years of advertising, he would have to point to the growth of research as that development. The restless, probing minds of the researchers will continue in the future to guide advertisers. Even more than today advertising men will ask, before making a final decision: "What does research say?"

One reason why future advertising men will look upon research as an indispensable advertising tool is that research will be surer of its techniques and, hence, its answers. There will be more qualitative research, and less of the quantitative (sometimes referred to scornfully as "nose-counting") research. Advertisers will be far more interested in the "why" than the "how many." One inevitable development is that the man who pays for the research—the advertiser—will know much more about research techniques in the future than he does today. The current typical advertising man is lost in the jargon of research. He views uneasily the social researcher who performs the research assignments. He is, more often than not, unable to argue successfully with the researcher's statistics or conclusions because, bluntly, he does not understand research. He knows only that there can be value in research. Thus, without having a solid understanding of the activity, he puts himself trustingly in the hands of those who, he has been told, *do* understand what they are doing.

The future advertising man is going to be more knowledgeable. He will know statistical method, research techniques. Of necessity, he will have a greater grasp of the language and methodology of psychology. Equipped with such background, he will know better how to evaluate research proposals or results. There will be little unquestioning trust in the technical ability of his research director, or of the outside research men called in to conduct research.

Where will motivational research fit into the future picture? Is the current passion for motivational research a form of mass hysteria such as flagpole sitting, Tom Thumb golf courses, and marathon dancing—the sort of thing that is taken up wildly and in mass, and then dropped with equal speed? It does not seem so. Motivational research will become a permanent fixture in advertising investigation. It answers a long-felt need to explore beneath the surface.

Undoubtedly, there will be many changes in the way motivational research is conducted. Use of this tool for advertising has really just begun. Presently, there are many crudities in the execution and interpretation of motivational research. Who really *knows* that the current methods of eliciting information are the best or that they are executed correctly? Do we know enough about focused group interviewing, or projective techniques such as free-word association, sentence completion, or picture responses? In the years ahead we will know much more, so much more that these techniques will be modified, or perhaps dropped.

It is not in the execution of motivational research, however, that the greatest reform will occur but in the methods for interpreting the results. A great weakness in present-day motivational research is that, given the same data, four different motivational research men may evolve four different interpretations. Disciples of Freud, Adler, and Jung—and many others—each shade interpretations in accordance with their beliefs. Variation in interpretations worked out from the same set of data is intolerable if the advertising man is to entrust huge sums to motivational research. Either such variation is eliminated or this form of investigation will have no more validity than many forms of modern media research that seem, oddly enough, always to arrive at a set of figures that support the sales story of the sponsoring media.

Speaking of media research: already attempts have been made to work out all-media yardsticks by which all media may be compared in terms of impact, and sales-producing cost. To this point, such yardsticks have been attacked bitterly for their alleged unfairness to one medium or another. Much talk has flowed regarding the illogicality of comparing "apples with oranges." Most of the argument has involved comparisons of newspapers and the broadcast media.

Criticism of the crude, prejudiced "yardsticks" thus far utilized is justified. Almost all the attempts that have been made to achieve a common media denominator have been made by persons affiliated with one medium or another. Despite the fact that the media themselves will probably never agree that an all-media yardstick can be achieved which will be fair to all media, such a yardstick will certainly be worked out eventually because media buyers, already hopelessly indecisive because of the profusion of media choice, will demand this aid to media decision-making. These media yardsticks will, in the enlightened future, give the advertiser an accurate, impartial scale through which he can figure, market by market, just which medium makes the best buy for him. Best of all, he will, through the use of the yardstick, make his media comparisons quickly. He will not be tortured, as he is today, with the indecisions that result from analyzing set after set of impressive and "impartial" figures presented by representatives for the different media—each set of figures, of course, demonstrating that the medium presenting them is unquestionably the best buy.

The foregoing discussion about the eventual use of media yardsticks should not carry the implication that in the future there will not still be questions for the media buyer. There will *always* be some questions. In the broadcast media, for instance, we will never know how many are actually listening or watching at any one time, nor will we ever know of those listening or watching how many are absorbing the message, nor how much impact the advertising message is having. There will, however, be much more use of simultaneous checking so that at any given moment the advertiser can know how many radio or television sets are tuned in. Despite the fact that the advertiser will know that great numbers of those people tuned in will not be watching his message, he will derive comfort from his knowledge of the exact number of persons who are at least exposed to his message. This knowledge will be his through the use of electronic switchboards in each city. Radio or television set activity will be flashed upon these switchboards in each city. A national advertiser will be able to check market by market exactly how many are tuned to his commercials. To help him further there will be a master switchboard that will give totals for the nation. There will not be, as today, a long wait to find out the patterns of set activity. With simultaneous electronic checking, an advertiser can make quick changes to bolster weak markets, or weak radio or television programs.

Subliminal advertising, under strict supervision, may well be used in the future. Despite the present furor about this use of persuasion, public opinion may gradually swing toward preferring this kind of advertising to the less subtle forms. It will be a long hard fight to overcome the feeling that subliminal advertising has sinister implications. Should the feeling be lessened, the networks and the Federal Communications Commission will work out a plan for the use of subliminal advertising that will permit the technique at certain times and for certain types of products.

Although the future of subliminal advertising is hazy, the use of basic advertising research, as differentiated from the current concentration on applied research, is not in doubt. Advertisers will come to realize that much value can come out of advertising research that seemingly has no direct application. Up to this time, there have been few in advertising willing to sponsor research that has no quick use by the sponsor. This situation will change just as it has in the area of product research.

One of the fields most needing such research is industrial advertising. Despite the great service performed by industrial advertising, and despite the fact that much of this advertising is in behalf of some of the great names of American industry, industrial advertising research has been negligible. Basic research has been almost nonexistent; applied research has been scant. The reason for this is obvious. Industrial budgets are small. At to-day's high prices for research, even a modest research project represents a disproportionate percentage of the advertising budget.

Even now, however, the attitude of the industrial advertiser is changing. He is becoming more research-minded. He is willing to spend for research. To serve him, more independent research organizations are entering the field. Publishing houses such as McGraw-Hill and Chilton are providing research help. Eventually, ways will be worked out to provide the industrial advertiser an opportunity for continuing-research on a cost basis within his means. The field is wide open at the moment for research organizations that can offer industrial advertising research at realistic prices —prices that are a far cry from the swollen prices now being charged for consumer advertising research. This same realism will be applied to the research performed for the low-budget advertiser of consumer goods who, like the industrial advertiser, wants research but cannot afford it at today's prices.

One factor that will help reduce research costs to a point where more advertisers can afford it will be the increasing use of automation by the researchers. Chilton Publishing Company's mechanically sorted and indexed cards designed to help advertisers locate industrial markets provide an example of the sort of automation that will be common in future research. With mountains of information recorded in card systems and available in minutes for the user, much of the costly labor will be eliminated. Although some start has been made toward the use of automation systems in advertising research, it can be said safely that progress thus far is tiny compared to what will happen in just a few years.

Just as this aspect of research may be hard to recognize a few years from now, so might it be difficult to recognize the advertising agency in the years ahead. Some of these changes have already been portended in the 1950's. One of them—the marketing agency concept—will continue to grow until the advertising agency does, in fact, become a marketing agency. It will not be surprising if, in the future, the name "advertising agency" is not wholly discarded in favor of "marketing agency." One pronounced effect of the change will be more stability for the agency field. A marketing agency, intimately concerned in its client's manufacturing, packaging, pricing, warehousing, and sales administration, will be much more of a partner in that client's business. Longevity of accounts will, therefore, increase since there will be much less experimenting with agencies. Gone will be the attitude: "Maybe it's the advertising that's to blame. Let's try another agency; maybe a new approach will help."

Today's trend toward bigger agencies will continue as mergers become commonplace. The marketing concept will fan the merger rush because the multi-city agency can better serve the wide-flung interests of clients.

Because of the marketing agency concept there will, also, be a gradual swing away from the traditional 15 per cent system. A marketing agency's wide range of services cannot be paid for through a rigid percentage system. As fee systems, or share-of-profits systems become commonplace, the 15 per cent discount will be looked upon as old-fashioned. Eventually, the system wherein the media have, in effect, supported the advertising agencies, will disappear. The agencies will work out their financial arrangements with the advertisers who, in turn, will pay the media.

While it seems certain that strong to mild changes will take place in all the media, especially in the areas of mechanical production and editorial or program format, it does not appear now that advertising in the media will undergo drastic changes. Newspapers will, for one, offer better printing, better paper stock, and more editions in order to cover widespread suburban markets, and different city sections. The most pronounced difference from today's newspaper advertising will be in the expanded use of color. Uniform color standards will be achieved from coast to coast, and all newspapers large and small will offer r.o.p. color of good quality on a daily basis. Since this will make newspapers much more attractive to national advertisers, we will have a revival of the national network for newspaper advertisers. This time, however, the network, remembering the sad experience of the 1940's when a network failed, will *make* the plan work.

Although little change can be seen for magazine advertising, or for the outdoor industry (outside of increasing restrictions and more use of three-dimensional posters) the broadcast media will experience some pronounced changes. Radio national networks, for one thing, will finally be dead. Regionals will survive and will be hooked together in case of national emergency. Complaints about programming will become louder until the Top-40 approach of today will pass on. Commercials will be less numerous and less insistent than they are today.

Commercial treatment in television will, likewise, be less annoying than today. As in newspapers, the most noticeable difference from today's presentation of advertising will be in the use of color. It is not difficult to envision the day when no commercial will be delivered in black and white. The selling power of television commercials will be increased. Competition, thus, will become that much sterner for newspapers and magazines.

Some form of pay-television will have been instituted which will mean that the viewing audience can have television with or without commercials. Despite the great dreams of pay-television promoters the system will have little effect upon commercial television. The latter will provide more intelligent programming, and less commercial saturation to offset the appeal of commercialless productions. Only a relatively small portion of the public will be willing to pay for television entertainment. Since that "small" audience will, nevertheless, number in the millions, it will be enough to make pay-television profitable for its promoters.

Videotape, a system that records both sound and pictures simultaneously on magnetic tape, will be used everywhere and by everybody. Because videotape offers such fidelity and because it can be played back immediately it will largely replace present-day filmed television—it may replace it entirely. Imperfections in any show or commercial being recorded can be edited on the spot. Tape commercials may be completed in one day that have, to this point, taken three weeks to run through film processing. Videotape will have great effect on the advertiser, the independent station, and the networks. While it seems doubtful, as some are saying, that videotape can destroy the networks, the latter must adapt their operations to its use.

One of the most important developments in advertising will be its increasing maturity. It is, today, still a youthful activity, but it has been learning quickly its place in our social and economic society—and the obligations entailed in deserving that place. Advertisers, especially the larger ones, are conscious of the power of advertising and of the need to use that power for the common good.

Increasingly, it is recognized that advertising must be scrupulously honest, that it must be in good taste, that it must not debase the language, and that it should avoid appeals to raw emotions in order to sell goods.

[72]

Advertising's important role in evening out the ups and downs of economic cycles is becoming recognized—a role that will become even more important in the future when the advertising men, and the economists themselves, more fully understand it.

An ever growing factor in America's social and economic life, advertising has already made significant contributions to our system. So long as that system continues in its present form, advertising will continue to grow and will continue to make its contributions. With maturity will come a knowledge of how to operate within our system in such a way that many of the irritations that have accompanied its growing period will be eliminated.

VII

Syndicates

ROBERT W. ROOT

THE FIRST STEP in sizing up the journalism of the future is to size it up correctly today. If one analyzes recent trends accurately, then he may hope not to go too far wrong when extrapolating the curves to 1970 or 2000. Were we to compare newspaper syndication today with four decades ago, for example, all of us would probably agree that syndicates now offer considerably more intelligent interpretation of events and a great deal wider variety of materials. It seems a safe guess that four decades from now the syndicated interpretation will be still more brilliant and the materials much more varied. Will we be right?

Maybe—but the catch is, not only that we may be wrong about the real trends of the recent past, but that even if we are right, the trends may shift. Second-guessing history is bad enough but second-guessing the future is worse. At the height of the enthusiasm for facsimile transmission a few years ago, it seemed certain that we would be getting our newspapers out of little machines in the living room by 1958; but that enthusiasm has been atomized; we still have carrier boys and will for a long time. In 1953, however, one would have been silly to predict that syndicates would before long be moving millions of words about space ships. In 1958 one knows that they are distributing just such millions. And so in 1963 it may seem absurd that, a mere five years before, anyone hesitated to foretell the creation of the new Space Correspondents Association to assure well-rounded coverage of the joint Earth-Mars fleet starting for the Milky Way. In short, as in the stock market, trends may go not only into nose-dives but into the accelerating spirals of a moon-rocket.

Today syndicates are strong and growing. The business "is an expanding and predominantly healthy one," said *Editor & Publisher's 32nd Syndicate Directory* (1957). "There has been an increase of 15 syndicates since the directory a year ago, bringing the total to 182 organizations which sell more than 1,700 daily and Sunday comics, columns, and other feature material to the newspapers of the U.S. and Canada." The directory took seventy-two pages to list the syndicates, their features, and their ads. Growth has also been the note of the annual reports of the news syndicates.

[75]

The United Press increased its clients by 230 and the International News Service by 249 during the year immediately preceding their merger as United Press International, in May, 1958. The total of clients of the merged agency was reported in the neighborhood of 8,000. Meantime, the Associated Press, which is organized as a cooperative, reported that its quite stable membership was 1,741 but that it had established new bureaus at Johannesburg and Bangkok.

The news syndicates continue their emphasis on interpretation. The last UP report before merger praised articles that "tell why an event occurred or that explain its meaning," and AP declared reporters in the Space Age "must background themselves educationally as never before in history." Canadian Press, in *(CP)—The Story of the Canadian Press,* a few years ago also promised "to probe deeper into the human forces that govern the political, economic and social life of nations." Knowledgeable observers like Frank Luther Mott,[1] journalism historian, and pollster George Gallup have been predicting more newspaper emphasis on interpretation.

Barring disasters, which have to be barred in crystal-gazing anyway, the syndicates themselves would forecast a bigger, brighter, better future, with more emphasis on explaining the meaning of events.

From the viewpoint of a critic interested in an intelligent, dynamic press, however, there are many reasons for pessimism about the future of syndicated journalism. The economic pressures on the development of syndicates are tremendous, and these have at least two bad effects. They push toward journalistic monopoly, and they drive down the quality of the product, making it synthetic, stereotyped, sensational.

Just as the trend is toward fewer and stronger newspapers, the movement will almost certainly be toward fewer, bigger, and more powerful syndicates in the news field. The validity of this analysis was underscored by the 1958 merger of UP and INS. Such a trend has been foreshadowed by newspaper consolidation in the cities. The competition of two or three papers in a city may produce more virile coverage than a monopoly. But as costs mount, maintaining competitive news staffs comes to be considered a luxury, and in most cities monopoly results. It is even argued that monopoly brings better coverage because city editors can concentrate on significant reporting instead of working up sensational headlines. Exactly the same rationalization would eliminate syndicate news-fighting.

Already the press has agreed to let one man cover some battles and

[1] "It seems likely that the newspaper of the future will be more and more concerned with interpretation. As it yields the 'flash' news and bulletins to radio and television, it will give more attention to orderly, departmentalized news for the record." Frank Luther Mott, *The News in America* (Cambridge: Harvard University Press, 1952), p. 216.

bomb tests for all American papers. Logic demands extension of the practice. In some foreign capitals, there is now no American newsman; would
it not be better to have one correspondent who would write for AP and
UPI under a cooperative arrangement? Why not a man who would corre-
spond for both from Belgrade? And if it works there, why not a single wire
bureau in Des Moines? Why not then perhaps in Washington? Why should
readers and advertisers (it will be argued) bear the high costs of two duplicating networks anyway?

Facts which have been reported since UPI was formed have high-
lighted the problem of avoiding consolidation of syndicates. INS was said
to be having annual losses of one to two million dollars, and UP was working on "low profit margins." "INS was unable to raise its prices because
of the competitive situation with UP and AP," said *Editor & Publisher*.
"Clients put up strong resistance with threats to drop the service."

The first reaction of the Justice Department to the merger was to
inquire whether antitrust laws were being violated. Representative Emanuel
Celler of Brooklyn declared, "It is essential in a democracy that there be
continued strong and healthy competition in the gathering and distribution
of news." Senator Estes Kefauver said the seriousness of the merger could
"not be underestimated." He urged that a temporary injunction be obtained
to stop it.

The flurry against merger was brief, however. *Editor & Publisher* ob-
served editorially that union of the services was "probably the best and the
only solution to the problems confronting them." The Justice Department
decided that there was no law violation, since one of the businesses was in
the red. In San Francisco, a cartoonist lampooned a hillbilly Kefauver in
coonskin cap, pointing ineffectually at a UPI teletype machine. Silent and
helpless, the public acquiesced. The news battle continued now between
two giants—perhaps more furiously than the three-way battle. But economic factors maintained on both a pressure to find a *modus vivendi* for
market-splitting if not outright union.

Antitrust laws may slow such further merger; but laws can be changed,
opponents can be ridiculed by the media, and consolidation can be explained as the only feasible way out. By the hard argument of ledger ink,
monopoly in the United States will probably be brought to the syndicate
business, as to other big businesses.[2] That is the danger of the next half

[2] A kind of law of diminishing monopoly may oppose this trend. The
fears that all newspapers would be joined in one or two big chains have so
far proved unjustified. However, there appears to be no economic reason why
a smarter Hearst could not keep on indefinitely buying newspaper properties,
for profit, power, and vanity. For such a man the purchase and consolidation
of news and feature syndicates might also be desirable.

century. By A.D. 2000 the question of syndicate consolidation in the United States may long since have been settled. The real debate then may be centering on whether the world's readers should now permit the creation of a single news cartel, to unite the American syndicate, Reuters, Tass, and the other dinosaurs remaining after decades of global news war.

As in some one-paper cities, the first effect of monopoly may be better service. But after the first years when editors are proving that syndicate consolidation was not so bad after all, quality will depend largely on the idealism of the men in power. There will still be good professionals on the job who will struggle against depreciation of quality. The competition of unbiased newsmagazines (if any) and of independent newsmen on television may help stave off deterioration. The newspaper reader is the only other force that might press toward high quality. Readers, however, are notoriously disorganized and ineffective. Reader pressure registers primarily in the money box anyway, and since at least the day the penny press started, newspapermen have cynically contended that a worse press, not a better one, was demanded by the vote of the mass readers' small change. The yellow press has always fattened on the vulgarity of the masses.

Intelligent readers in many one-paper towns also know well the decline in quality, the sheer sloppiness, which comes as owners (perhaps in the second or third generation of a family's control) shift the image of themselves from editors to businessmen like other businessmen. The monopolist whose interest is greater in the balance sheet than in the news budget not only vitiates local coverage but saps the syndicates; like the buyer of cotter pins for a factory, he wants the cheapest merchandise that will do. For example, he does not want to pay for many foreign correspondents. Such hard facts of news life were demonstrated again and again by the sales efforts of the manager for Worldover Press (now World Around Press), an interpretive news syndicate where I was an editor. One publisher put the point bluntly in refusing to buy. He conceded that it was a good service, that it would improve his paper, that price was no factor. "But," he told my boss, "what the readers of our paper are getting now is good enough for them." Why bother to improve if you don't have to? No doubt he would also be content with a few scraps from a future world news cartel.

Under attack from the apathy of such owners in one-paper towns and from the budget demands of the syndicate, quality will tend to erode. News executives will be pushed to cheapen the product; the cheapening will be less as our schools (especially our journalism schools) succeed, will be greater as the syndicate monopoly falls into the hands of those who amassed or inherited their capital in channels cut off from the best news traditions.

Syndicates

Even if monopoly of the syndicates is avoided, however, at least three trends toward lower quality promise to continue and worsen. Syndicated material will become (1) more conventional; (2) more sensational; and (3) more propagandist.

1. Syndicated materials will more and more take on the synthetic slickness of the mass-produced, the prefabricated. At best, the gains of syndication are offset by the ironing out of individuality. Writers' styles may become more and more bizarre, but ideas become more and more conventional.

Critics of mass culture in the West have long pointed to the tendency of media to conform and to reproduce conformity. The trend appears to be worldwide. For example, I did not need to know Turkish to be struck by the similarity of three recent Istanbul papers, to each other, and to our own papers—down to the photographs of American movie stars. Today's "other-directed individual" of David Riesman and "the organization man" of William H. Whyte, Jr., are in part the result of outside molding, but in turn they demand the conventional, the noncontroversial, the safe. The mass-molded feel most secure with molds. More and more, like the politician speaking the day before election, the syndicate will have to please all the other-directed organization men. As syndicate power and monopoly increase and the public-utility aspect grows, indeed, the syndicate men will be as eager as the telephone system to give offense to no client, no government official. The result will necessarily be as insipid as a TV comic's script.

The introduction of the Associated Press stylebook a few years ago—salutary as it was—symbolized the way conformity must follow syndication. All the papers jump into line with the stimulus. Even without that book, however, the spread of the teletypsetter would have brought style conformity; the keys at the news central regulate capitalization and punctuation, and individual papers have to go along or introduce confusion. Ideas, however, will tend to conform too, like commas, under the punch of those keys. There is a newspaper word for the result—the stereotype.

The teletypesetter has already brought us close to the centralized production of newspaper stereotype plates. One's imagination does not have to be very lively to see how technology and automation can bring us closer. Why should editors in cities of 25,000 or 50,000 struggle with typography when nationally known experts in the graphic arts can send makeup instructions on teletape? Why can't experts in New York decide what stories should be played up, and why indeed can't experts write and transmit the heads for all the papers? Newspapers look more and more alike anyway, someone will point out, so what is to be lost if high-priced expert editing is provided by the syndicate—and at less unit cost too?

[79]

Only the requirements of local news display stand in the way of such centrally produced front pages. The old United States weekly (and many papers in Germany today, incidentally) bought partially printed pages ("ready-print") and stereotypes ("boiler plate") to help fill their pages cheaply; if it will save money and therefore produce more profit, ingenious newsmen may discover more modern ways to combine local coverage and editing-by-syndicate. Local stories might be plugged for street sales with news posters as in England, while the home subscriber could learn to find his local news in an inside section—as in many Sunday papers already today. Or a big banner over the name plate could direct the reader to the big local story. Gallup has predicted that future "make-up will be designed less to attract front-page reading, and more to get cover-to-cover, above-the-fold and below-the-fold reading"; books, magazines, and newspapers all have a tendency to grow more alike, as Mott has pointed out. So perhaps the newspaper of the future will look like two magazines, one made locally, the other a kind of up-to-the-minute cross between the *Reader's Digest* and *Life,* produced by electric impulses from New York. By 2000 it is very likely that at least several pages of the paper in Los Angeles and of another in Minneapolis will be as identical as if they had come from the same New York facsimile transmitter.

If newspapers retain more typographic control than that, their conformity will nevertheless be great. Under the impact of syndication, it already is. Many stories within the country have the same on-the-one-hand-but-on-the-other-hand flatness—dead-pan objectivity at its worst. At the same time, "interpretation" permits more subjectivity in foreign coverage. Careful reading of stories about Khrushchev, Nasser, or Nehru will reveal in most of them the same viewpoint—yes, "slant." Coverage of the satellite launchings, which have been called "a race," has been about as dispassionate as the football releases of a college athletic department. Syndicate interpretation, that is, takes the attitude approved by the current, Washington-conditioned state of public opinion. So from both old and new kinds of reporting, we get the same conformity. As the national community is tightened by still faster transportation and communication, syndicate editors and writers may in 1980 or 1990 trim as close to the Washington "party line" as the weekly editor today sticks to the views of the small-town Chamber of Commerce.

Feature material too, while seeming more varied, may in fact become more and more alike. Canned editorials were bad enough. But today syndicated preachers set a somewhat sentimental religious pattern for the nation, and syndicated lovelorn editors give dating advice which is hep in all corners of the nation—with psychiatric help, yet! We have syndicated book reviews and syndicated TV criticisms. Soon, if they have not already, syndicates will be offering predigested cultural opinions so that the reader in Phoenix as well as in Detroit will know what to think of a lately discovered Van Gogh or a new American symphony. The more it will seem to change, however, the more all will be the same.

2. Syndication promises not only to become more synthetic and conformist but more sensational. For centuries newsmen have used sex and crime to titillate readers. But a long-term trend towards bigger, better sensations, as toward bigger, better news generally, is unmistakable. What was a sensational scoop at the end of World War I would be tepid today; there may be a Victorian reaction, but the Hollywood cheesecake of 2000 promises to make the Bikini beauty look like a Gibson girl (though the nature of the editorial ingenuity required for that is not clear at this time). Television, controlled by government, will probably not be able to get much more violent or sexy, so that the newspaper perhaps will be able to compete with TV best by sensation. Thus, under the paper restrictions since World War II, competition drove the popular newspapers of Britain into greater daring and vulgarity. With the literary novel, the paperback, and even the slick magazine today pioneering new sexations for the printed word, the American newspaper syndicate appears to have this real future advantage over television. Unless it is careless, the press will get worse much faster than TV!

3. The monopolistic and leveling pressures of economics will be matched by political pressures, which are harder to assess with certainty. The conservative who sees a worldwide trend toward statism will be sure that in 2000 the American press will be run from Washington as Tass is run today from Moscow. We can all probably agree, from the experience of the last generation, that government will become even more important to newspapers than it is today. As editors fought the Star Chamber in 1630, editors in 2000 will surely be battling bureaucrats at all levels of government, to uncover secrets and keep the public informed. Big Syndicate may succeed against Big Government better than the fragmented press succeeds in Washington today (although this would depend upon a human will which may be lacking if competition disappears). The halfhearted and unsuccessful effort of the press in trying to get the State Department to permit American agency correspondents to go to Red China is a sad portent, however, to the old-fashioned liberal.

Government in turn will employ more public relations men with more Mimeographs to get its story out. We have to stretch our imaginations only a little to visualize a government syndicate—the "Domestic Information Service"?—pumping handouts directly into newspaper offices by teletype "to let the taxpayers know what is going on." The tendency of the press today to hold down reporting staffs and their pay, and to rely on publicity releases more than was dreamed a few years ago, of course increases this possibility.

In short, the really cynical observer can draw a very pessimistic picture of the evening paper as the other-directed organization man of 2000 sits down to read it. He will get a soft mishmash of news and features, propaganda-tinged and sex-tainted, spoon-fed to the most moronic denominator in the population and seasoned by owners more interested in money than pure information and by government officials perpetuating themselves through hidden persuasion.

Fortunately, however, the prognosticators of gloom have usually proved wrong in history. Things are bad but maybe never quite as bad as the gloomiest expected. Some hopeful trends exist, and if they do not portend a roseate future, they may at least counterbalance the degenerative factors.

As in the past, one of the great pushes for improvement will be better schooling. In a few decades, almost everyone of average or better intelligence will have a college education. Improvement in the press does not appear to be directly proportional to average years of education, but even those who are disappointed at the progress made during this century would concede that newspapers publish much more solid, thoughtful stuff than in 1900.[3] The better educated public of 2000 will demand still more. Syndicates will have to meet the demand or others will.

As the years pass, we will get more interpretation, as already suggested. The proportion of foreign spot news will also increase further (Mott has pointed out that the percentage of foreign news in the nonadvertising "hole" of a group of American newspapers went up from 3.1 to 8.2 between 1910 and 1950). As travel abroad increases, more and more of the interpretation also will be about events overseas, especially in Asia.

The erosion which interpretation is tending to produce on objective reporting may result in more outright editorializing in the news columns. As in today's interpretive stories we have critical editorializing about Russia—for example, unglossed cracks about Khrushchev's taste for vodka—we will have it about our then enemies, unless international libel law rapidly develops. If our school system is kept for education rather than propaganda, however, readers may become more impatient than now with

[3] The cover story of *Time*, the "profile" of the *New Yorker*, the "most interesting characters" of the *Reader's Digest*, and the more recent personality sketches even of the *New York Times* indicate developing interest in the news as the story of great men. The approach appeals to intellectuals as well as the modestly educated. Syndicates have long had features on people in the news, but as newspapers take on magazine aspects, the emphasis on personalities should grow.

tepid or biased opinionizing. To please a more educated population, and to build up circulation, syndicate editors may encourage stimulating debate among interpretive writers. Today's columnists, largely chairbound, provide the appearance of political variety within a narrow range near the political center (Westbrook Pegler may perhaps be overlooked); but syndicates of the future may keep interpretive correspondents arguing, from more extreme right or left positions, in copy from Tibet and New Guinea about developments on the world's frontiers.

Higher education coupled with more leisure will stimulate more syndicated copy in the area labeled culture. There will be more but also more perceptive articles about travel and photography. There may be more penetrating columns on religion and even theology and philosophy. At the same time there will be syndicated guides to reading in the classics, articles about getting more enjoyment from your chamber music group, and how-to-do-it material on Sunday painting, sculpture, and composing.

Will our syndicates of 2000 be so heavy with interpretation and culture that scholars will look back with sad head-shakes at the state of the *New York* Sunday *Times* in 1958? To conclude that they will, I think, would reveal a superficial understanding. Then as now, the egghead will have to look for what interests him in a deluge prepared for the dunderhead.

But this too suggests a hope for other signs of higher culture and I. Q. in the press. Won't the larger numbers of educated and cultivated be able to demand and pay for a specialized press? Probably. Today we have publications on hi-fi and the theater, and the magazine promises to proliferate into all sorts of more obscure cultural specialties. This possibility increases as we consider the probability that technical progress will lower the cost of good printing and adequate paper. The work of the Mimeograph and of the Varityper-Multilith combination today suggests how much cheaper production might become.

The Big Press and the Big Syndicate will take advantage of lower costs, and their power can become more entrenched. But at the same time, the little free enterpriser may find it more possible to take his shoestring and start his weekly cultural paper, or even his little liberal daily, than at any time since 1900. The very bigness of the syndicate business will doubtless stimulate reaction and even revulsion. Those who are independent-minded, politically or culturally or religiously, may start their little papers in almost every city and region. Who cares if circulation is only a few hundred or thousand, if a copy can be produced for only a cent or two, as in "the good old days"? When old syndicates merge, specialized new syndicates may spring up to serve the little papers, as syndicates and newsletters dealing with religious, business, labor, and science news developed in the first half of this century to serve readers with special interests.

We must finally consider whether the portents of syndication are bright or gloomy for solving our most urgent problem of the second half of this century—international understanding and peace. Idealists, including journalists, have argued that avoidance of war depends upon the international flow of pure, true streams of news, unmuddied by propaganda. "If there is ever to be understanding among peoples, if there is ever to be comity between nations, it must be built on a far more solid foundation of truth and fact and confidence," Robert McLean, AP president for twenty years, said recently.

It is not a new AP theme. In *Barriers Down,* hardheaded Kent Cooper, former manager of the Associated Press, complained years ago that the old European news monopolists "brought under their control the power to decide what the people of each nation would be allowed to know of the peoples of other nations and in what shade of meaning the news was to be presented." That was bad. But the AP in 1934 broke that monopoly, for its idea was "that international news, which generates actions upon which the fate of nations depends, should not be sold or bartered, restrained, suppressed or tainted: in short, that the urge to have news agencies traffic in international news for profit was not a wholesome procedure." Other AP-like national cooperatives of newspapers have developed, and it is tempting to conclude that the news flow will be clearer and purer.

However, in the perspective of history, this development of the AP between the wars at the expense of the British-French-German news monopoly is seen to parallel the emergence of the United States as a major world power and the decline of Western Europe. Perhaps the shift of press power is only part of a trend towards a new concentration, as the Western military power center has shifted from Europe to the Pentagon. Maybe a bigger monopoly will now rise on the ruins of the old.

The forces of nationalism push for continuance of news syndication along the present power bloc lines—Reuters for the British, Tass for the Russian sphere, and so on. But there are also strong supranational and international forces which raise in the press sphere, as in the political, the question whether one world can be built without excessive centralization at the expense of national sovereignty.

A conservative writer such as Robert U. Brown, editor of *Editor & Publisher,* could write recently that, while people may not want to give up national sovereignty, "maybe the free press of the world will find a way." He cited the increasing exchanges among editors and the international press organizations springing up. "In these groups there already is visible a greater understanding of each other's problems, both economic and political," he said. "Some of this is bound to be reflected in their individual news columns."

[84]

If that vision is somewhat ambiguous, others go further toward "internationalization." The writer of a UNESCO brochure, *News Agencies, Their Structure and Operation* (Paris, 1953), pointed out that the big news agencies are national; he deplored that the "news they collect and distribute is chosen, written up and presented almost entirely by United States, British, French and Russian journalists," and these men "inevitably judge and present views from the viewpoint of the country of which they are citizens." The trend has been toward free-for-all scrapping over the news. But, he asked, won't newsmen have to come to "international cooperation" in news collecting? Perhaps a news agency could be attached to the United Nations, he suggested, or a world cooperative agency could be created.

Cooper had pointed out that newspapers used to distrust each other's news, and so they created a cooperative agency which would provide news acceptable to papers of varied views. The check-and-balance is missing, of course, where all the papers share the same bias, as on some economic questions. These same considerations press, on the one hand, toward development of supranational syndication which would provide unbiased international news acceptable to editors of different nations; but on the other hand they warn of the straightjacket lurking in the shadow of anything approaching cartelization.

If there is a danger from greater internationalization, there is also some sure hope in it. Under pressure from the International Press Institute, transmission rates in Asia have recently been reduced; the flow of news, already increased, will grow further with such international pressures in the future. Under IPI sponsorship, French and German editors have been getting acquainted, and in 1958 ten German editors, aided by French editors, studied the Algerian question on the spot. If Germans and French can get together, one can hope that Russian, Chinese, and Western editors may one day get acquainted too. On the one side our concern may be that badly conceived, monolithic development of world syndication may put us at the mercy of Big Brothers high in earth's power structure; but on the other, our hope can be that the greater international influence may purify the flow of information and increase, not merely our understanding, but our empathy.

When the varied trends are mingled, then, what picture emerges? Optimistic or pessimistic? Both. By 2000 we will have bigger, perhaps monopolistic syndicates, and most of their output will be synthetic, noncontroversial, sensational, superficially varied but actually vapid and conventional. The demand for interpretation, foreign news and cultural help, however, promises to be so great that the Big Syndicate or new little syndicates (and probably both) will have to meet it.

Fortunately, the future is not controlled by fate, Calvin and Marx notwithstanding. Tomorrow is not closed and sealed. Just which trends continue and which disappear will depend upon the way men resolve the tensions generated among the conflicting possibilities.

Today the glacier of economics and politics is grinding so inexorably towards low-level, mass conformity that the man or woman of 1958 may feel he can do little to preserve values. Still, those of us now living can teach those of younger generations to appreciate, to want, to buy, and to create journalistic products which are finer and sounder than older generations have demanded. By doing so, we may scratch the glacier, may help prepare the way for some future syndicated materials vastly better than today's.

VIII

Photojournalism

FREDERIC A. DEMAREST

IN 1842 A PHOTOGRAPHIC RECORD, using the Daguerreotype process, was made of the destruction of Hamburg, Germany, after a four-day fire. This, one of the first news photographs ever produced, was made only three years after Daguerre had introduced his photographic process to the world. Thus was ushered in one of the most powerful mediums of news reporting the world has known.

In 1859, the first aerial photograph, a picture of Paris, was taken from a balloon by the French artist Nadar. The photographing of the earth from above its surface, therefore, is not a recent development swept in on the wings of the air age, as we might suspect, but rather an accomplishment forty-four years before the Wright brothers made their historic flight.

Less than twenty years after the first news photograph was produced, Mathew B. Brady, in 1861, appeared on the battlefield of the American Civil War with his now famous "What-is-it" wagons. This pioneer in the field of photojournalism all but abandoned for awhile his very successful and world-renowned portrait business to finance the most extensive photographic coverage of a news event ever attempted up to that time. At the end of the war, Brady and his many teams of photographers covering every major battlefront, had exposed on the battlefields, in the ruins, and in the army camps, over 7,000 negatives. It is little wonder, therefore, that his coverage combined with that of Alexander Gardner and the many other photographers, North and South, resulted in one of the most comprehensive pictorial war coverages of all time. This, despite the difficulty encountered in producing the photographs.

Brady used the wet plate process, which required sensitizing the glass plate in his portable "What-is-it" darkroom wagon immediately prior to making the long exposures with a bulky camera mounted on a tripod. The exposure was followed without delay by developing the still wet plates right on the field of battle before the plates had time to dry.

The heavy glass negatives, usually 8 inches by 10 inches in size, were then carefully packed in the wagon to prevent their becoming damaged from the journey over the rough terrain of the roads and the battlefields. After their safe return to the studio, prints were prepared from which were produced the many woodcuts that appeared on the pages of *Harper's Weekly*.

This was the method employed less than a hundred years ago in getting the news pictorially to the public—a far cry from the method in use today.

It must be said in passing, however, than even under the conditions described, Brady, Gardner, and the other Civil War photographers were successful in producing photographic interpretations of war which are today considered classics; photographs which graphically portrayed, perhaps for the first time, the real horrors and agonies of war; photographs containing a certain aesthetic quality which elevates them above the plane of mere records.

Today, a photojournalist selects from a wide assortment of films, sensitized months previously in spotless, modern, air-conditioned plants, the particular one best suited to his needs. After loading his camera, which is considerably less bulky and clumsy, and much more maneuverable than Brady's, he takes an action-packed exposure at speeds upwards of one-one thousandth of a second, returns the exposed film to the laboratory where trained technicians rush it through the development and printing processes, and send it to the engravers where a reproduction is made that appears in the very next edition of the newspaper. Or he might even develop the print right in the camera, within seconds after the exposure, and then within only a matter of minutes have a reproduction of the photograph in the living rooms of millions of homes across the country via television.

From the fragile wet plates to the sixty-second print, from long exposures to high shutter speeds, from bulky cameras to hand-held miniatures, from handmade woodcuts to halftone reproductions; all this in less than one hundred years.

Today the photographer is no longer burdened with heavy, unwieldy cameras, traveling darkrooms, breakable glass plates, slow wet emulsions, long exposures. Instead, today's photographers have what seem to be the ultimate in equipment and supplies—cameras so small they can literally be concealed in the palm of the hand, lenses so fast and optically perfect that no subject matter seems impossible, shutter speeds so rapid that action traveling too swiftly to be caught by the eye can be "frozen" on the film, emulsions so sensitive that even recording the invisible is possible, and photoelectric exposure meters whose sensitivity measures the light regardless of its intensity.

Still, it is true that the photographer must learn how to use these pieces of equipment and supplies if he is to be skilled in the medium. Only after he has mastered the techniques is he free to concentrate on the content of his photograph.

Within the past decade alone almost unbelievable progress has been made in the photographic field. The sensitivity of monochrome emulsions has increased manyfold. Today films with exposure indexes of 1600 or higher are no longer considered uncommon. The emulsion speed of color film has increased twenty times during the same period. Instantaneous exposures in full color are now possible with only the light from an ordinary household match supplying the illumination. Negative color photography, permitting retouching and other controls not readily possible with positive color film, is now more than acceptable when good quality color prints for either advertising, layout, or reproduction are desired.

Electronic flash, now widely used as a means of illumination, makes possible the recording of moving objects traveling at unbelievably high rates of speed. The bullet ejected from a gun can be "stopped" in mid-air by the camera.

Photographs in the depths of the sea as well as thousands of feet above the earth's surface are common. There seems no limit to what the camera can do.

Yet even today the photographer is often not completely free from his equipment or from tradition. He is not free to create and interpret as he wishes. He may be burdened by his equipment, or he may be burdened by tradition from creating the masterpiece he is capable of producing.

But what of tomorrow? Are there improvements still to come?

Already there is a new film being marketed, whose present use is limited to duplicating and slide making, which after exposure to ultraviolet light can be developed immediately utilizing nothing more complicated than the heat generated by a simple match—no chemicals, no darkrooms, and best of all, with no grain.

Tomorrow full color prints will be produced in the camera in a matter of seconds. Negative color, permitting the production of excellent quality full color prints, black-and-white prints, and color transparencies will be greatly advanced and widely used, perhaps even to the exclusion of the present popular reversal color processes.

The principles of magnetic tape recording and of electrically charged plates will have a revolutionary effect on still photography. Chemical processing will be entirely eliminated in many instances.

Advancements in electronics will make many of today's camera adjustments obsolete, freeing the photographer to concentrate even more attention on subject matter. Film emulsions will be more sensitive and less grainy, in both black-and-white and color films. Newspaper reproductions in color will be common both in advertising and in illustrating, and will be superior to those in use today. Magazine illustration will be wholly, or almost wholly, in full color.

Photographs of outer space, taken in outer space, will be familiar scenes in the newspapers and periodicals. Long before man ventures into space, however, the camera will have recorded many of the wonders that will greet him when he gets there. By the year 2000 man will have known for some time what that side of the moon which he has never seen really looks like. He will know because a camera-armed rocket will have circled the moon and will have returned carrying photographs of it. Perhaps even by the year 2000 photographs taken on the surface of the moon by man himself will be appearing daily in the press. Certainly there can be no doubt of the indispensability of photography to the exploration of outer space. No longer will space "Columbuses" be unable to explain the mysteries of their "new worlds" to the people at home, for the explorers will return armed with graphic proof of what they have seen. If these space explorers find life on the other planets comparable to that of human life on Earth, photography may well play the major role in informing these inhabitants of distant horizons of life here on Earth; at least until some other form of communication can be established.

Photography of outer space will not minimize the importance of photography at home, however. There will continue to be stories and events for the Earth-bound photographer to record and interpret.

If automation of photography is going to play such an important and impressive role in the photojournalism field of the future, the question might very sensibly be asked, "Will there any longer be a need for the trained photographer?" The answer is that the unimaginative, unartistic, and noncreative photographer will not be needed. In fact, by the year 2000 he will have ceased to exist, for there will be no place for him.

There will be a very definite and very important need, however, for well-trained, skilled photographers; trained and skilled in the arts of seeing, selecting, composing, and interpreting. Although there will always be a place for record photographs, the important use of the medium of photojournalism will be to interpret and to communicate the impact of the news to the populace.

The selection of subject matter cannot be handled electronically. The composition of a photograph, the selection of camera angles and lighting patterns must be performed by a sensitive eye—one trained to "see." For a photograph is produced not by the camera, or by the physical action of light upon a sensitized surface alone, but also by the eye, the mind, and even by the heart of the artist.

Many of the photographs of the Civil War, mentioned earlier, are masterpieces, not because of the equipment with which they were taken, equipment long considered antiquated by present standards, but because they were made by sensitive artists, artists who selected that which to them had real meaning. Through this process of selectivity and sympathy for what he was photographing, the photographer was successful in capturing for all time the mood and emotion involved in the scene before him, and to communicate to the millions upon millions who have viewed these photographs something of that which he felt when he recorded it.

Even though almost a hundred years have passed since Brady walked the fields of Gettysburg recording the aftermath of the debacle which only hours before had taken place there, and Alexander Gardner made his memorable photograph of the dead Rebel Sharpshooter, these photographs remain as classics of war's futility. They are no longer merely records of the Civil War, rather they are interpretations of the effects of war in general; all wars regardless of the time or place.

The many great photographs of World War II, of Korea, of Hungary, of everyday life, are moving because the artist behind the camera selected that which was important, concentrated on that which told the story, and by so doing interpreted the events so forcefully that they are successfully communicated as living experiences to all the world, regardless of the language barrier. For photojournalism which does not communicate does not deserve space in modern news media.

The future promises an abundance to the artist with the camera. The simpler the techniques of camera adjustment, the freer will be the photographer to create. And create he will for the camera was made for creating. The photographs of the future will be filled with examples of human emotion and understanding, for the equipment will release the photographer to concentrate on this aspect of the medium. Happiness, sorrow, despair, disillusionment—all will be successfully captured on the film.

There will still be a demand for records, but even here the photographs will be more than a simple record. The famous photograph of Winston Churchill, for example, made by Yousuf Karsh of Ottawa, Canada, during World War II is a historical record of a great leader. Yet it is much more than just a record of the facial features of a man. In addition it is the study of a man's character and soul; a visual account of a man which reveals more than volumes of words could begin to reveal. And because it does reveal much that is beneath the surface as well as on the surface, it is a much more valuable document.

There will be many more such records as this in the future. For the future offers a great challenge to the photojournalist. But at the same time it offers an abundance of opportunities for meeting the challenges.

Regardless of how advanced the equipment of the future may be it cannot do the communicating. That must be done by the artist. For the

[91]

camera is to the photographer no more than what the brush is to the painter, or the pencil to the writer. By successfully and harmoniously integrating the use of advanced techniques with his creative talents the photographer is going to capture and present the events of the future in a thrilling and expressive manner. In many cases the photographs will be unlike any seen thus far by man. For this reason tomorrow will be impatiently awaited by photojournalist and viewer alike.

IX

Mass Communications Research

WILLIAM P. EHLING

TO SPEAK OF MASS communications research is to refer to an activity whose short history does not extend much beyond two decades. Compared with such highly developed sciences as chemistry and physics, which trace their origins back more than three centuries, mass communications research appears to be a mere fledgling.

This, however, is not necessarily a meaningful comparison. We need but look about us to see that many of the scientific disciplines we take for granted today are relative newcomers. The science of modern economics looks back to David Ricardo in the late eighteenth century; sociology begins in 1839, when Auguste Comte first conceived the term *sociology;* what is accepted as present-day psychology is really a product of the late nineteenth and early twentieth centuries. Scientific medicine with its amazing accomplishments in surgery and its endless variety of wonder drugs is less than fifty years old; and to pick still another new area of development, meteorology and climatology have made the most important advancements within the past thirty years.

Mass communications research is a child of the age—the age of scientific analysis which characterizes the first half of the twentieth century. It is a product of the explosive expansion and wide application of scientific and empirical methods of investigation to a host of uncharted areas in our physical, biological, and social worlds.

An interesting parallel exists between the scientific study of mass communications and the scientific study of the weather. First, both have been developed within recent times; second, and more important, both are concerned, not with single or isolated factors, but with a collection of complex phenomena which go to make up a particular natural *system*. In short, both focus attention on the *relationship* of various factors which constitute the total pattern of behavior under investigation. In both areas of inquiry, rigorous methods of measuring, recording, and analyzing the dynamics of a system are employed—whether the system be the sum total of all conditions responsible for changes in the weather or the sum total of all conditions involved in the sphere of mass communications.

Someone once defined a sociologist as a person who is constantly startled by the obvious. Sociology has also been referred to as the science of explaining what is self-evident in words no one can understand. In a sense, all scientific disciplines are tinged with this desire to know more about the obvious and to develop a more technical, more precise vocabulary to describe the phenomena under study. While the layman looks for simple answers to complex questions, the scientist (or those engaged in scientific research) cannot ignore the complexities of definitive answers to simple questions. To the layman, rain is obviously "caused" by rain clouds, and he feels that even a child can quickly learn to recognize a thunderhead as the source of lightning, thunderclaps, and a heavy downpour. To the meteorologist, the cause of rain is not that simple, and he is the first to admit that the *cause* of rain is still shrouded in some mystery, requiring still further investigation and research. Thus he speaks guardedly and technically of the "causes of coalescence and hence precipitation." Nor is he fully certain as to how the lowly hailstone is formed. In other words, while the average individual simply wants to know whether it will rain or hail, the scientist wants to know *why* it rains or hails.

By the same token, there are indeed few people in the United States who are not personally familiar with the various instrumentalities of mass communications—newspapers, magazines, radio, television, and the like. And practically everyone in contact with these media has opinions about them—their content, their impact on audiences, their effectiveness as purveyors of information and their proper role in society. But much of the reaction to, and opinions about, mass media are impressionistic responses to the superficial trappings of this or that medium. This is natural and to be expected. The average individual is more interested in what the headlines of his evening paper say or what will be shown on television tonight than what impact these headline or TV programs are making on the general reading or viewing public.

On the other hand a student of mass communications—be he social scientist or a researcher in journalism—tends to focus his attention on the total mass communications *process*. He is more curious about the particular functions of mass media in this process and in the role these media play as social institutions than in their immediate content or physical characteristics. He is fundamentally more interested in *why* media make an impact on an audience than in the mere fact that they are making some kind of impact.

There is a world of difference between a person engaged in mass communications research and the professional newsman or media technician.

[94]

The latter feels he knows from past experience and training what a particular audience expects and how that audience will react to what is being communicated. The main concern of the practicing journalist centers on what will attract and hold the attention of a reading, listening, or viewing public.

The researcher is less inclined than his practicing colleague to rely on intuition and impressions (as sound as these may prove to be) in these matters; he seeks, instead, empirical and measurable data from which he can derive precise and workable generalizations (to describe a particular phenomenon). Unlike the layman or even the professional, he is more guarded in his statements about the impact of mass media on the audience and more cautious in searching for single causes about this or that response evidenced on the part of the reading, viewing, or listening public.

Answers to such questions as what kind of information is being conveyed by mass media, in what amounts, to whom, and with what impact are anything but obvious or self-evident. Social scientists know that people who live together in a common polity develop patterned ways of distributing information. These patterns of information-flow, however, interact at many points with other patterns of social behavior—status, wealth, power, literacy, urbanization, and homogeneity. This interaction process of information-flow with other social values forms a system, and institutional variation in one segment is accompanied by regular and determinate variation in the others.

An essential aim, then, of mass communications research is to determine the kind and degree of systematic relationship between communications and other types of institutional or social behavior. This is by no means simple. If we are to talk about the future development of mass communications research, it is important that we have some idea of the methodological and theoretical problems encountered in this area of scientific inquiry.

Problems of Research Scope and Content

In 1957 Wilbur Schramm reviewed in an anniversary issue of *Public Opinion Quarterly* the progress made in journalism research during the past twenty years. He summarized the change in these words:

> The development in these twenty years is a most dramatic one: from almost wholly nonquantitative research, to a fairly even balance between quantitative and nonquantitative; from an almost exclusive preoccupation with the methods and viewpoints of the humanities, to a concern with methods and problems of the behavioral science as well; from a view of the printed media as the shadows of the great personalities, to a view of them as part of the social process, and from a local or national to a worldwide focus.

If we project into the future the line of development in journalism research since 1937, several important factors emerge.

First, we should expect a continuing interest in mass communications as a process—but a process which will be more closely studied in terms of both its quantitative and normative aspects. We can anticipate, therefore, an ever-expanding body of knowledge of what *is* (or what in reality constitutes) the actual relationship of this process and the total social structure on the empirical level, and what *ought* to be the relationship between the communications process and society on the normative level.

Second, we should expect within the near future the emergence of a fairly sophisticated theory of mass communications. Theory construction— a vital factor in the advancement of research—is only now being introduced in communications studies. We can anticipate far-reaching consequences as new research approaches are integrated with new theoretical concepts and methods of empirical investigations are meshed with methods of formulating productive generalizations.

This is merely another way of saying what Ralph D. Casey wrote in his "The Challenge to Journalism Education" (*Journalism Quarterly,* Winter, 1955):

> No crystal ball is required to predict that in the next decade the schools of journalism whose policy it is to appoint highly trained personnel will continue to make important contributions to communication research. . . . In the next decade, journalism schools will encourage, support, develop research; will use research findings and will set research standards on a level with those in the behavorial sciences and other established disciplines.

Not all research in communications, of course, will be conducted within the confines of schools of journalism; we shall continue to see widening interest in communications research on the part of psychologists, social psychologists, sociologists, and those working in such areas as group dynamics, human relations, and public opinion research. Nor will all research be of a narrow, quantitative type. There appears good reason to believe that a closer relationship will emerge between quantitative and nonquantitative research, with a corresponding elimination of those investigations which are regarded as "realistic, large, important, woolly and totally inconclusive" and those which, while systematic and conclusive, are "small, artificial, and trivial."

Admittedly, such future developments do not appear very startling at first blush, and yet there is every reason to feel that the greatest promise for major advances in mass communications research will come in the wake of this slight shift in emphasis and the broadening of theoretical concepts mentioned above. If this is true, we should see even more dramatic research developments in the next twenty years than we have seen during the past two decades.

This optimistic note, however, should not blind us to some of the serious procedural and substantive problems which inhere in the general area of communications research. In talking about the future of research in journalism or mass communications (at least for the purpose of this chapter), it might be fruitful to point to some of the more troublesome problem areas which are in need of investigation or to which more systematic attention should be given in the future.

There are three areas which call for scrutiny. The first is that of clarifying the distinction—if, indeed, one actually exists—between "journalism research" and "mass communications research." Interestingly enough, we persist in speaking of "journalism education," but we seem to have abandoned the term *journalism* in favor of *mass communications* when it comes to research, even when this research endeavor is part of the journalism education enterprise. Is there any sound, logical basis for this switching of terminology or are we merely engaged in meaningless semantics?

The second area is concerned with the concept of *mass*. Precisely what do we mean when we use this term? To what or to whom does this word refer? This is a crucial question, particularly when we employ *mass* as an adjective with such words as *media* and *communications*. When is a particular medium a *mass medium* and when is it not? What is *mass communication* or how do we distinguish between communication which is *mass* and *nonmass?*

Lastly is the area dealing with the differences between impersonal communication and interpersonal communication. We frequently refer to impersonal communication (usually intended to include such communication channels as newspapers, radio, television, and so forth) as a mere social extension of interpersonal communication (sometimes inaccurately called oral communication). If this is true, at what points are the two joined or where does one leave off and the other begin? And in the final analysis, what is the significance of making such a distinction between apparently two different types of communications?

Journalism Research and Mass Communications Research

Even a cursory review of research developments in journalism and mass communications shows that the major advances have been largely methodological; the contribution of the past two decades has been that of increasing the quantity of empirical data but not the quality of theory. It would appear that we lack not only a general theory, but also basic operational concepts, of such widely used terms as "journalism" and "mass communications." It is not that we are in short supply of textbook definitions of these terms; if anything, definitions are legion, creating a confusing bramble of terminological disputation. What we need, instead, is a set of generalizations which belong to what Merton (1957) has called "theories of the middle range, logically interconnected conceptions . . . limited and modest in scope," which have the virtue of quality, utility, and logical soundness, rather than grandness or the all-embracing structure of a major synthesis.

While admittedly synthesis of knowledge is desirable, we need not strive for some master scheme into which every problem may be fitted neatly; rather we need to rise above the present molecular level (wherein we find fragmented data or *ad hoc* definitions) to a level where consolidation of information can take place and be fitted into a workable theoretical structure.

Objectives of Journalism Education. Lest this appear unnecessarily academic or even irrelevant to the main issue of practical research, we need but call attention to the concern that journalism educators, thoughtful editors, and other media executives have about the primary function and responsibility of journalism education. Casey (1955) in his essay on journalism education states categorically that "first and primary, journalism education needs to arrive at some determination of its objectives." He notes that many journalism teachers accept, sometimes too casually, the restricted role of merely training students in certain skills they will require as communications craftsmen and appear self-satisfied in the knowledge that a certain number of graduates obtain jobs with newspapers, radio-TV stations, advertising agencies, or some other media. Moreover, he questions the propriety, if not the logic, of attaching the term *communications* to an academic division formerly called a School of Journalism, and raises the question as to whether a journalism school has a fundamental understanding of what is required when it operates under the label of *communications*.

The real significance of Casey's comments is to be found in the fact that there are no quick and ready solutions or answers to the problems he reviews and the questions he raises. Technological change as well as developments in the so-called areas of "communications research" have had a profound impact on the thinking of journalism school administrators and journalism educators. The stable concepts of journalism evolved before World War II are not adequate enough to permit us to *exclude* perfunctorily such new ideas as public relations or communications from the province of journalism, and yet these newer ideas of communications, human relations, or public relations have not been sufficiently developed to require us to *include* them in journalism. This is another way of saying that we have reached a point in growth where some are wondering whether *journalism* is any longer a sufficiently meaningful term to describe the diversified academic activities or expanding educational objectives of many college or university divisions we have come to know as schools of journalism. Others are concerned lest we abandon the term in favor of some other, even less precise and educationally more confusing, label.

Change in Research Perspective. Journalism education and research in journalism are not disconnected activities; the substantive content of one has an obvious effect on the development of the other. The attitudes and the orientation of journalism educators toward "journalism" determine to a large extent the type of research they pursue or have their graduate students pursue. They also determine whether a formal research center will be established within the framework of a journalism school and the type of sponsored research such a center will accept. Conversely, those engaged in research usually solicit certain types of courses, particularly at the graduate level, which will develop the skills they consider essential for the sort of research in which they are interested; the result is that we shall continue to see, as we have seen in the past, a host of statistical, methodological, and behavioral science courses introduced into the graduate journalism curriculum.

Since World War II, partial solution has been to employ the term *journalism* to refer only to activities on the academic side and the term *communications* to refer to research activities. There has been virtual abandonment of *journalism research* as a meaningful term.

In considering the research process the confusion of terminology is more than a mere question of semantics; it is a problem of necessity—a necessity of knowing, for the sake of research direction, whether there is an essential difference between "journalism research" and "mass communications research" (or, more inclusively, "communications research") and, if so, whether this difference can be justified by a clearer definition of objectives and a fuller substantive understanding of content.

One way of looking at the problem is to see the two terms as alternate ways of referring to the same kind of activity; another is to see them as referring to autonomous divisions of research with overlapping subject matter; still another way is to see one as subordinate to the other and concerned with specific aspects, which are essentially part of a larger frame of reference.

Expansion of Journalism Research. If we turn back to earlier concepts of journalism or look at the result of early research in the field of journalism, we find a fundamental preoccupation with the operations of the *press,* perhaps, more specifically, the working operations of newspapers. This restricted view gave way in the late 1930's to a broader concern with all *printed* media. We find that biographical and historical studies of great journalists and great newspapers were now being supplemented by studies in readership, content analysis, contextual organization of written material, readability and reading ease, audience reaction, and, more recently, the measurement of meaning.

This growth and development in research can easily be traced through the work of Lee, Mott, Emery, and Smith in the history of the press; Schramm, White, Bush, Teilhet, and Swanson, as well as the American Research Foundation, in readership studies; Hughes, Kingsbury, Hart, Lasswell, Leites, and Berelson in content analysis; Flesch, Gunning, Klare, Buck, and Taylor in readability; Lazarsfeld, Katz, Klapper, McPhee, Schramm, Hovland, Berelson, Janis, Merton, Wiebe, and a host of others in the effect and process of communication.

These and other investigations treated not only newspapers but also a whole variety of publications and other printed material including popular magazines, books, house organs, direct mail pieces, employee handbooks, et cetera. With the advent and growth of commercial radio, and later television, research quickly branched out to include studies in the sample survey of audience reactions, listener preferences, program content, and media effectiveness. These studies, in turn, were extended to a whole range of newer media, grouped into such general categories as "audial," "visual," and "audio-visual" channels of communication. More recently, we see efforts to build even newer classifications in order to deal with the increasing variety of mass media in terms of their role, i.e., "informative," "interpretive," "persuasive," "critical," and "entertaining." Thus, journalism research as it moved out of the 1940's into the 1950's could no longer be concerned, either logically or pragmatically, with printed media alone. One needs but review articles in the *Journalism Quarterly* since 1945 or read a current list of journalism theses for evidence of the breadth of interest and the variety of research activities found in schools of journalism on the part of graduate students and faculty.

Changing Character of Mass Communications Research. Reinforcing this broadening of interest among journalism educators and researchers was the growing concern of advertisers with consumer behavior, and of public opinion pollsters with voting behavior. Both groups were interested in the size, composition, and reaction of mass communications audiences—the former to assess the impact of mass media on the consumer's buying behavior and the latter to determine the influence of mass media on the decision-making process of the electorate. Since this interest was coming from such diversified sources as marketing research personnel, political scientists, sociologists, social psychologists, journalism educators, public opinion pollsters, not to mention advertising, radio, magazine and newspaper executives, it became easier, if not more accurate, for all interested parties to refer to their investigations as mass communications research rather than journalism research; and the somewhat unwieldy term, *mass media of communications,* soon had wide currency among scholars, researchers, practitioners, and laymen alike.

Moreover, the Lasswellian formula of "who says what in which channel to whom with what effect," which came into use just before World War II, provided a convenient five-fold division of communications research: control analysis, content analysis, media analysis, audience analysis, and effect analysis.

This classification provided considerable impetus to research in mass communications through a logical division of labor in the research vineyards, through employment of categorizations which cut across the physical and technological differences of various mass media, and through the creation of the impression that mass communications research was rapidly developing into a separate discipline with several quasi-autonomous subunits.

This divisional approach, in addition, had the advantage of making researchers more aware of the complexities of the mass communications *process,* thereby providing new insights into the intermediate steps which "intervened" between mass media stimulus and the individual's response. But in this process, attention was turned from mass *media* as *instrumentalities* of communications for reaching the *mass* to the effect of mass media in influencing opinions and attitudes. The result was that researchers became more interested in the general communications process than in the individual differences of mass media or in the distinction between what was meant by mass media and nonmass media.

As journalism research (particularly as conducted in journalism schools) broadened its interests to include all mass media (in terms of both structure and process), mass communications research (particularly as conducted outside journalism schools) shifted its interests from composition of audiences of various mass media to the general communications process. Amid these changes, the distinction between these two types of research activities today appears to have become more apparent than real.

We can derive from this the conclusion that we should see in the near future a deeper concern with, and a more intensified study of the problems created by the present bifurcation of thinking about research as it relates to journalism. We should see more discussion as to whether we are dealing with an essential difference or merely a terminological difference between *journalism education* and *mass communications research,* and, if the former, whether the difference is one of different approaches to the same subject matter.

If journalism as an academic division of education as well as a professionalized activity in the market place is to benefit fully from the systematic and disciplined investigations into communications, some common connective link must be clearly established to permit a meaningful integration of journalism education and mass communications research. Moreover, we need to ask ourselves whether the so-called integration of research in journalism with that in the behavioral sciences is a one or two-way street— whether it is less an integration than a drift of journalism educators into the behavioral sciences.

Before we can feel certain that true integration exists we need to know at what points and under what conditions the objectives of research in journalism (or in mass communications) are compatible with, or coupled to, the objectives of journalism education or professional journalism. The disturbing fact is that at the moment, the latter objectives are neither precise nor consistent.

This problem raises additional questions. Does journalism contain a central core of meaning that can define areas of research uniquely related to *journalism* (as distinct from mass communications, group relations, sociology, and the like), and thereby give impetus and direction to investigations which should be admitted solely and logically into an activity called journalism research? The answer to this question will tell us under what circumstances we should retain the term journalism research or abandon it in favor of mass communications research. It should also go some distance in clarifying whether journalism education is primarily, if not exclusively, an enterprise for the training of craftsmen in literary and writing skills, or whether it is an endeavor requiring, in addition to an understanding of technical communications skills, a knowledge of the institutional structure of mass communications, special techniques, characteristics, and limitations of mass media. It should also tell us what kind of research activities will permit the plowing back into journalism of fresh information, new concepts, and/or a synthesis of communications research findings.

By the same token, we should see a clearer formulation of what is meant by mass communications research—both in terms of its scope and content. Here, too, a clear definition of objectives is now lacking. To draw on the work of other disciplines—psychology, sociology, and statistics, for example—to provide new insights into the central problems of mass communications is one thing; to become so engrossed in the conceptual schemes, research designs, and orientations of other disciplines so as to make the study of mass communications an incidental activity is quite something else. To state it differently: to study some aspect of mass communications in order to gain a better understanding of a social or psychological phenomenon is not the same thing as studying social or psychological phenomena so as to have a clearer insight into the structure and process of mass communications. The resulting data may be similar, but the approach is uniquely different. Those committed to the study of mass communications, especially journalism researchers, may well ponder their point of departure.

The implications of these problems for the future are obvious. Moreover, the future direction of research in journalism will be determined to the extent that those in journalism engaged in research can clearly define the focus of their research efforts and can avoid becoming displaced behavioral scientists with only a polite interest in journalism.

Concepts of Mass Media and Mass Communications

Solution to the above problem may well have to await greater clarification of the role and characteristics of *mass media* and a more systematic formulation of a theory of *mass communications*.

The direction taken by theory and research of the past in dealing with problems of mass communications media has been influenced by two types of activities: first, efforts to develop general categories of analysis (i.e., "content," "audience," "effect," and the like) which could be applied to all mass media whatever their specific differences in physical appearance or technological operation, and, second, attempts to investigate the broader social implications of the mass communication process itself.

Both approaches sought to provide a more adequate understanding of what constituted the substratum of a particular mass communications *system*; seeking such an understanding was another way of recognizing the need for concepts about, and corresponding research into, what is both fundamental or deep and yet *common* to all media of communications. As important as such broad concepts may be, it does not necessarily follow that they will help distinguish between *mass* and *nonmass* media; more likely, such concepts tend to blur the differences, treating, instead, all communications channels as mass media.

Concepts of Mass and Mass Media. This kind of problem goes back to where Louis Wirth (1949) left it when he stated that "since we shall speak of our society as a mass society and of the communication that it involves as mass communication, it behooves us to depict the characteristics of the mass." Indeed, even after the passing of a decade, it still "behooves" us. In spite of Wirth's helpful efforts to spell out these characteristics, we still have not moved far beyond an heuristic definition of "mass." While Wirth's description invited further analysis, the amount of study has been limited. What has been said about the mass seems only to point up conceptual differences and the difficulty of arriving at a definition which will clarify what is meant by such terms as "audience," "crowd," and "public" when related to the concept of mass.

If we are still some distance from an adequate definition of mass, we are even further away from a systematic description of *mass* communications or *mass* media. We have not progressed much beyond the common-sense notion of mass as meaning a "large aggregate of people" and mass communications as meaning "communications addressed to a large cross-section of a population."

Under the circumstances, we can still wonder indecisively whether an annual report of a private corporation circulated to a million stockholders once a year is any less a mass medium than a newspaper which publishes daily but circulates to only 80,000 subscribers, or whether a regularly published magazine, financed and controlled by a governmental agency like the United States Information Agency and intended for mass consumption overseas is less a mass medium than a community controlled and financed educational television station which, while optimistically appealing to all, actually reaches only a certain specialized group of viewers.

Part of the reason for the lack of an appropriate definition of mass media as we noted earlier is due, in no small part, to the orientation of researchers studying mass communications and their preoccupation with the categories of audience, content, and effect analysis. As Katz and Lazarsfeld (1956) have pointed out, these categories of analysis, while useful for some research purposes, are misleading or inhibitive for other purposes because they obscure "the fact that, fundamentally, all of communications research aims at the study of effect." In other words, these categories of analysis reflect areas of *concern* which basically are attempts to impute effects by means of investigating some more readily intermediate factors with which effects may be associated.

It is true that by shifting the focus of our attention from mass media as instruments of communications to mass media as a communications process, it was possible to divide up a given communications act into manageable segments which *eventually* could be analyzed independently of the media through which it passed. But in so doing, it became increasingly difficult to find a conceptual scheme which would permit us to look at the total communications process at once and analyze its relations to, or role in, the entire social system.

Moreover, the terms mass media or mass communications have been made to cover such different concepts as the content of a newspaper or a television program, or an aggregate of people performing the technical operations of a business enterprise, or a social collectivity with its own peculiar institutionalized patterns of behavior, or a specialized form of human communications operating within the larger social communications process.

It is not particularly helpful to be told, in one breath, that mass media are dependent upon mass patronage, and, therefore, must transcend in content and mode of presentation the peculiar interests and preoccupations of special and segmental groups, but in so doing become "as near everything to everybody and hence nothing to anybody as it is possible to be"; and, in another breath, that "it is upon these mass media that to an ever increasing degree the human race depends to hold it together" and, therefore, mass media are rapidly becoming the "main framework of the web of social life."

The problem is not that these assertions are untrue; rather the problem is one of having too many varied and essentially different meanings assigned to the same term. It has been said that it is easy to generalize when knowledge is not specific or to formulate definitions when the body of data is limited. Today, problems of definitions and generalizations in the field of mass communications research are indeed far more complicated than they were two decades ago; and it is becoming obvious that the restricted criteria of yesterday are no longer appropriate to give us working concepts of mass media for tomorrow.

Research Implications. The future implications which these problems have for research are many and varied. Should we focus our attention primarily on the *process* of mass communications within a larger social context, then by definition any medium—be it an individual or some physical or mechanical gadget like a teletype machine, a memorandum, an annual report or newspaper—may have affixed to it the term *mass,* just as long as it acts as a link in the total mass communications process. What is lacking is a certain preciseness to permit separating the parts from the whole. Should we, on the other hand, begin with the mass *media* themselves, we find that an analysis of their varying characteristics does not lead us to a clear idea of what we mean by *mass* media. To say that any medium may be considered to be a mass medium if it has attributes such as "swift transmission of information," "low unit cost," "appeals to heterogeneous groups," and "high entertainment value" only seems to be clouding the issue with terminological difficulties. Obviously these attributes do not apply equally or logically to all such physically and mechanically different media as newspapers, magazines, radio, television, motion pictures, and books.

It may be argued that the solution to the problem is to be found in a clearer understanding of the concept *mass.* But here, too, we encounter difficulties. The rudimentary or commonsense notion of mass as used in communications seems to imply merely that mass communications can be distinguished from other types of communications by the fact that it is addressed to a large segment of the population rather than to a few individuals or to some particular interest group. However, as Freidson (1953) has pointed out, this notion also carries with it the assumptions of time and a physical channel—that is, the notion assumes some technical means of transmitting the communication and a system of transmission which permits the communication to reach all the people composing the mass simultaneously.

This basic notion of mass appears implicit in the earlier writings of such students of mass communications as Lazarsfeld and Kendall (1949); it was amplified by such sociologists and social psychologists as Blumer (1946), Wirt (1949), and Wiebe (1952). They all viewed the mass as made up of people who were anonymous, heterogeneous, unorganized, and spatially separated—in short, an aggregation of individuals with "no social organizations, no body of custom and tradition, no established set of rules or rituals. . . ."

The question immediately arises whether such an atomic concept of the mass, as it is related to mass communications, squares with findings we already have about the behavior of people identified as members of a mass medium's *audience*. In other words, can such an audience be truly referred to as *mass?* In probing this problem, Freidson made several important observations. First, he pointed out that when we examine an individual member of an audience, we find that his behavior is of a decidedly different type than might be expected if he were a solitary member of a mass—that is, he does not act alone or independently of his social environment.

Second, members of an audience select their mass communications content under the pressure and guidance derived from their experience as members of a social group, and, in fact, their response to mass communications is a part of their social behavior; and, finally, mass communications are absorbed into the social life of local groups to which the responding individual belongs. In addition, he noted that while one can *describe* an aggregation of individuals as a "mass" or a "national audience" without reference to the organized groups that compose it, one cannot *explain* the behavior of its members except by reference to the local audience to which they belong.

Viewed through the framework of social groups, *mass media* takes on a different meaning than it does when viewed as a technical instrument or even as a corporate enterprise through which it is technologically possible to disseminate communications to large numbers of anonymous, solitary individuals making up an amorphous group called the mass. The same is true for the meaning of *mass communications,* which, as a process, is more than the mere flow of messages (content) from some individual (issuing source) through some disseminating instrument (media) to an aggregate of individuals (audience); rather it is a particular type of social relationship—an interaction process between members of a social group and certain kinds of media which play a specific social role within an organized human behavior system.

This leads to a second conclusion. If we are to make advances in the development of a systematic theory of mass communications, steps must be taken toward a better understanding of the nature of the human group and the specific role of particular media in the social process. Under the circumstances, we should see in future research efforts more widespread utilization of sociological concepts in order (1) to provide a better understanding of the character of the social enterprises that organize, produce, and maintain mass communications and their media; and (2) to define the character of the particular type of human associations we call "audience" in relation to other groupings, such as "mass," "crowd," and "public." We also should see efforts to analyze more thoroughly the kind of images people assign to particular media which act as their primary sources of communications. Such contributions will serve as important sources of fruitful hypotheses, illuminate specific areas in need of research, and make the application of specific research techniques more appropriate and more accurate.

New Concepts of Impersonal
and Interpersonal Communications

Freidson's efforts to anchor communications research in group life was a forerunner of the more definitive work of Katz and Lazarsfeld, who constructed a more elaborate theoretical model of communications to take into account factors of interpersonal communication intervening between the mass media message and the response of members comprising the mass media audience.

Development of Two-Step Flow Theory. Until 1940, it was assumed that mass media, particularly the press, exerted direct influence on the attitudes and opinions, and, therefore, on the behavior of people. The only question seemed to be that of deciding whether this influence was "good" or "bad," with debate waxing hottest in the area of partisan politics. This basic assumption came in for some critical review during the administration of Franklin D. Roosevelt when more and more daily newspapers seemed to line up in opposition to the Democratic administration but with seemingly little effect on the electorate's determination to return Roosevelt to the White House. A number of tentative explanations were offered to interpret, if not to explain away, this apparent waning of mass media influence.

It was not until the Erie County voting study reported by Lazarsfeld, Berelson, and Gaudet in *The People's Choice* (1948) that some light was shed on this problem. Analyzing the decision-making process of citizens during the course of an election campaign led the authors to suggest that the flow of information through mass media may be less direct than was commonly supposed. Instead, the authors felt, influences emanating from mass media might be received first by "opinion leaders" who, in turn, acted as secondary influence sources, passing on what they read or heard to their associates, who regarded them as their primary communications channel. This view established the hypothesis of "the two-step flow of communication."

This hypothesis implied a network of interconnected individuals through which mass communications is channeled in patterned ways, and clearly stood in opposition to the notion of an audience as a mass of discrete, unorganized individuals linked directly to media but not to each other.

Contributions of More Recent Studies. Efforts to verify this hypothesis with empirical data have led, since 1941, to a series of studies conducted by the Bureau of Applied Social Research of Columbia University —a review of which is presented in an article by Katz (1957) in *Public Opinion Quarterly*. The studies later led to a comprehensive analysis in the book, *Personal Influence: The Part Played by People in the Flow of Mass Communications.* These studies included Merton's analysis of interpersonal influence and communications behavior in Rovere (1949); the Decatur study of decision-making in marketing, fashions, moviegoing and public affairs, reported by Katz and Lazarsfeld (1955); the Elmira study of the 1948 election campaign reported by Berelson, Lazarsfeld, and McPhee (1954) and, finally, a study of the diffusion of a new drug among doctors by Coleman, Katz, and Menzel (1955).

These studies, in extending the theory of two-step flow of communications, introduced a number of important modifications and new insights. Comparing the findings of these studies, we are presented with several salient points.

First, personal relationships—as channels of communication through which influence is transmitted—affect the decision-making process of individuals more directly than mass media—thus underscoring the social integrative effect of interpersonal communication. Second, the effectiveness of interpersonal influence actually reflects the homogeneity of opinions and actions in primary groups—thus, emphasizing the important role played by social groups, as a channel through which mass communications flows to group members and as a framework against which people respond in selecting communications. Third, in this process, mass media must be viewed as playing diversified, although specific, roles which have an important function in the flow of mass communication—pointing up that a given decision is not influenced solely by one type of communications (mass media communications) or another (interpersonal communications) but rather by different types of communications at different stages of decision making, i.e., "different media play different parts in the decision-making process and take patterned positions in a sequence of several influences."

The place, then, of mass media, opinion leaders, and the social group in the total mass communications structure appears to be closely bound together, and, therefore, far more complicated than earlier theories have suggested.

The implication of this conclusion on mass media research seems to boil down to this: the influence of mass media communications must first pass into, or be absorbed by, a particular social group and move through the "influence sphere" of individual opinion leaders before such communications will reach and have any effect on less interested or less active members of the group.

Problems of Measuring Effect. To ignore the complexities of this communications system and the interrelations of impersonal and interpersonal channels of communications can lead to oversimplified or contradictory conclusions in studies of the effects of mass communications.

Klapper makes this point clear in an article in *Public Opinion Quarterly*. Although optimistic about the possibility of consolidating much of the diverse and unrelated findings which have accumulated in this field during the past twenty years, he, nevertheless, admits that research data on the effects of mass communications has now reached a "stage of profusion and disarray" which has created pessimisim about bringing order to the field among both interested laymen and research experts.

The problem is not simply one of improving the reliability of research techniques, nor one of finding newer methods for sorting "true" data from "false"; rather, it is a problem which turns partly on methodology and partly on theory design. Methodologically, we have been hampered by the narrowness or inappropriateness of the problems studied, by the manner in which factors or variables have been abstracted from the whole process, by the selection of inadequate techniques to qualify data, and by the limitations imposed by these and other methodological problems on our ability to generalize from incomplete or contradictory data in order to construct a more systematic theory of mass communications—or to answer larger social questions. Theoretically, we have been more interested in collecting quantitative data than in organizing such data; in this process, we have often proceeded with vague or misleading assumptions, not the least of which was the assumption that effects of mass communications could be studied in isolation, or that it was possible to trace a direct cause-and-effect line of action from a media stimulus to the individual's response, or that we really know what we mean by "mass media" or that the communication process could be easily segmented into such categories as control, content, media, audience, and effect.

Problem of Reconciling Theory and Methodology. The problem which calls for future attention may be divided as follows: first, that we develop the necessary understanding and skills toward the proper and effective use of research tools which are now available, with a corresponding grasp of the theoretical implications and limitations of these tools; and, second, that we organize and relate existing knowledge about mass communications in a manner permitting the construction of generalizations, hypotheses, and postulates which can lead to a more adequate theory of the function, process, and effect of mass communications.

At first blush, it would appear that what is needed to solve some of the problems reviewed above is more penetrating and rigid research. In reviewing the activities of the past, Klapper recognizes that the simple quantitative approach is not enough.

> We shaped insights into hypotheses and eagerly set up research designs in quest of the additional variables which we were sure would bring order out of chaos, and enable us to describe the process of effect with sufficient precision to diagnose and predict. But the variables emerged in such a cataract that we almost drowned. . . . It is surely no wonder that today, after eight more years at the inexhaustible fount of variables, some researchers should feel that the formulation of any systematic description of what effects are how effected, and the predictive application of such principles, is a goal which becomes more distant as it is the more vigorously pursued.

The strategy of the future, then, seems to be one of bringing theory in closer relation with methodology and empirical data; in short, they must be made to progress together if we are to uncover new phenomena, develop new concepts, and uncover and reject mistaken ideas.

This brings us to a third conclusion. The most fruitful path for the future is in the direction of erecting a mass communications model which would take into account and organize into a working scheme, specific characteristics of impersonal communication, as well as such mediating variables embedded in interpersonal communication as group membership, audience predispositions, personality patterns, flow of personal influence and the like. But in abandoning the path of "seeking simple and direct effects of which media are the sole and sufficient cause," we must guard against excessive theorizing, which tends toward vague and untestable abstractions. Progress to date has provided sufficient empirical data to permit the establishment of tentative generalizations; but the resultant conceptual scheme has also pointed to gaps as well as benchmarks against which future research may guide itself.

There is a need, then, for theory and additional research to explore further the proposition that mass media functions amid a nexus of other influences; the important thing for the future is to isolate and delimit these other influences, study their differences and how they are interrelated in the communications process. Additional studies are needed to demonstrate that the mass media of communications possess essentially unique characteristics and specific capabilities, distinct not only from the other, but also from those of the interpersonal communication channels of primary associations, peer groups, opinion leaders, and the like. It is also important to see, within the large social context in which mass communications operate, how and why distinct characteristics of individual media engender distinct effects.

In short, as we seek to account for a known occurrence and to assess the roles of the several influences which produced it, it will be important to distinguish between impersonal communications and interpersonal communications in a manner to permit the distinctive characteristics of each to be interrelated in a meaningful manner.

Additional Areas of Research Activity

Up to now, we have confined our attention to some broad problem areas out of which one may expect the emergence of new theoretical considerations. Admittedly, a close interrelationship exists between defining the nature and scope of mass communications research, organizing empirical data into fruitful generalizations, and the construction of research designs. Under the circumstances, no sharp line of distinction can be drawn between problems dealing with the objectives of mass communications research as a special discipline and problems of method and conceptualization embedded in scientific research in general.

The problem areas treated above, therefore, should in no way detract from the importance of the more immediate and basic methodological problems to which solutions are now being sought. These problems point to the possibility of new developments occurring with the continued refining of existing and the construction of new techniques of measurement and methods of analysis. Thus, we can anticipate more systematic coding procedures in content analysis and scaling methods in the study of attitudes and opinion. We can look to new advances in survey design construction, topological procedures, and modes of index construction, not to mention the utilization of more rigorous statistical and mathematical procedures, such as probability models for analyzing time changes in attitudes, latent structure analysis, newer methods of scalogram analysis, including the H-technique and W-technique, as well as other techniques of multivariate analysis that have been advanced by Anderson (1954), Lazarsfeld (1955), Guttman (1954), Stouffer (1952), and Simon (1957), to mention but a few working in this area.

Nor can we ignore, on the theoretical side, the emergence of new conceptual models, constructs and other theoretical schemes in the various disciplines of psychology, social psychology, sociology, and anthropology, and their eventual impact on the research activities in the general area of mass communications. We are reminded of the general excitement caused by Shannon's information theory, which provided such new concepts as redundancy, entropy, channel capacity, and networks; or the introduction of such notions as "gatekeeper," action system, reference-group, as well as the relationship of informal communication behavior and group cohesion and the co-orientation model of a two-person communications system elaborated by Lewin (1951), Parsons (1951), Festinger (1953), Schachter (1953), Merton (1957), Homans (1950), Newcomb (1955), and others.

As we review the research efforts of the past twenty years, we find that an impressive amount of work has been done in the process-effect area of mass communications research. Because of the richness and variety of empirical research, we are, as Klapper (1957) notes, on the "brink" of being able to organize apparent anomalous and contradictory findings and to proceed toward developing a more sophisticated and fruitful set of generalizations about the processes of communications effect, factors involved in the process, and the direction which effect typically takes. This movement toward a more comprehensive theory of mass communications, coupled with the fact, as Hyman (1957) points out, that "we stand close to a sound theory of opinion formation" holds promise of even more vigorous research effort into the newer "areas of neglect," with the hope of seeing the emerging generalizations molded into a more organized body of knowledge.

On the other hand, if we look at mass media in terms of social institutions, we should see a growing interest in the sociology of mass communications—viewed historically in terms of changing institutional patterns extended over time, or contemporarily in terms of an ongoing social process spatially extended but related to the same general dynamic.

Such an approach would partake not only of sociological, psychological, and political theories, but also of conceptions emerging in fields like administration and organization, group dynamics, and human relations.

Research with this kind of broad orientation should lead to more meaningful and qualitative answers to normative questions concerned with the responsibilities of mass media of communications in society, implications of future changes in the ethical-legal principles of freedom of the press and the right to know, and the impact of economic restraints and governmental regulations. It should also provide answers to such empirical questions about mass communications as the process of policy formulation and decision-making, the nature of organization structure, delegation of authority, planning and control, dynamics of personnel training and supervision, centralization and consolidation, mass media interaction, differentiation of roles or social functions, system of value-orientation and the cultural pattern of ideals and beliefs.

In reviewing areas in need of research, one can only repeat Schramm's words:

> In the realm of the history and sociology of journalism we need an adequate social history of the press in America, a history of mass communication as a social institution, a good study of the economics of mass communication, and an analysis of the workings of mass communication organizations—the internal networks, the decision-making systems, the interactions of policy and function. We have as yet no adequate picture of media personnel, their training, their jobs, their feeling about their jobs, their financial and other rewards, their codes of responsibility. We still have no competent study on a national scale of the performance of our press in an election campaign.

Interest in these areas is already in evidence and the future paths of research are being reflected in such endeavors as the study of policies affecting news selection (Cutlip, 1954), a psychometric study of editors (Jones, 1957), the "opinion-leader" role played by certain types of newspapers in the process of standardization (Breed, 1955), work activity of certain types of editorial personnel (Gieber, 1956), attitudes of readers to newspapers as social institutions (Nixon, 1954), responsibilities of mass communications media (Schramm, 1957), to mention but a few of the increasing number of studies appearing in current literature.

These studies point to an expected accumulation of systematic investigations and controlled experimentations in which a greater variety of extramedia variables being studied will be built into more complex research designs. Moreover, they promise a greater clarification of basic concepts of mass, mass media, and mass communications as well as a more precise definition of the role of research in journalism.

X

A Summing Up

ROLAND E. WOLSELEY and WESLEY C. CLARK

THE READER OF THIS BOOK by this time will have discovered some points of differences between the various authors. This is to be expected, for the men who wrote these chapters come from diverse backgrounds and are concerned with different interests. But the remarkable thing is the general picture of change which emerges, changes which are for the most part generally agreed upon. All of the authors see that there is a greater need for more communication and for more meaningful communication if the world is to survive in an atomic age. And all of them see substantial changes in the newspapers, radio, television, magazines, and other media. Yet all of the authors see substantial obstacles in the way of the kind of communication which will prove most helpful.

The changes which they foresee are not revolutionary, rather they are evolutionary, building upon the established foundations of the communications media already in existence. No author, for instance, foresees any great new development in the media comparable to the revolution sparked by the electronic advances of the first half of the twentieth century. To these authors, there will probably be no comparable introduction of anything like television or radio, merely refinements of the present systems of communication.

As these authors foresee the future, the problems which face journalism tomorrow are problems caused by increasing population, and by the consequent increasing governmental controls. Out of this complex of forces come the problems of the gathering and dissemination of news, of news selection and of news rejection.

There are, to be sure, some apparent paradoxes to be found in the forecasts of these authors. Many of them see fewer newspapers, more concentrated control of fewer media outlets. Others see a burgeoning of the communications industry. These are not irreconcilable differences. They come about because the authors are talking about different parts of the communications media.

Inevitably the pressures of population and of circumstance will make for more control and more concentration in the bigger communications outlets. These same pressures will raise the threshold of attention for these media, so that in general they will appeal generally to more and more readers. This raising of the threshold of attention will have profound effects upon the nature of politics and perhaps even upon the structure of government. Yet at the same time the threshold of attention is being raised by all media, there will remain the need of people everywhere for attention, for prestige, for recognition. To meet this need there will be an ever increasing number of publications and media outlets catering to special groups and to special interests. Some of these will outgrow their early purpose and move into the area of general news.

This process might be described as that of gradual growth and decay. As organizations grow they will become stratified, structured and rigid, and yet, in a free world, where freedom of choice is still of some value, the ingenuity of men and women will again and again find ways to escape the rigidity of bigness whether it be private business or government. It is largely out of this free interplay of ideas that will come the solutions of problems caused by population and other pressures. And again in these circumstances is to be found the hope of the future in the communications field.

And what of the future of journalism education itself?

A profession which has been transformed as forecast by most of the authors of this book will change substantially the nature of journalism education. Thus the shape of such education, a half century hence, will depend considerably on what happens to journalism. And we have seen what may occur. If the various media become more and more mechanized, instruction will have to take that into account. No one now, for instance, seriously tries to teach practical courses in newswriting without typewriters, although in the early years of journalism education it was the rare school or department that possessed such writing machines. Newspapers lacked them, hence schools thought they could do without them also.

Schools of journalism will be larger both in enrollments and in physical plant. With the anticipated rise in the population it is inevitable that educational institutions will be both more numerous and also physically larger. Since the trend in journalism is toward more and more research and mechanization, it is likely also that journalism schools as such will depend heavily upon other schools on the campus for part of their instruction. It now is common to leave the teaching of the liberal arts and certain technical subjects to these colleges. A journalism which might be largely electronic in its physical aspects, for example, would demand that the journalism educators require their students to take at least limited courses in the colleges of engineering and science as well.

There would be no point in duplicating the equipment possessed by physics departments, for instance, any more than there is in offering instruction in mathematics or foreign languages, since it is available in colleges of liberal arts.

Along with this great sharing of students of journalism with other colleges of the universities will come a balancing activity by the schools of journalism themselves. A number of their courses will become all-college or all-campus subjects; special courses also will be offered as services to all students.

Liberal and vocational education will be more than ever intertwined because the broadly educated journalism student will be the only one who can survive in a country with as high a level of education as American citizens will possess by century's end. Therefore, journalism school curricula will emphasize the responsibility of the schools to help the ordinary citizen to appreciate the meaning, value, and importance of a free communications system. The school of journalism will expand its services to the point where the rank-and-file student will be helped by it in making intelligent use of journalism. Courses in how to read or use his newspaper or magazine, whatever its physical form by the year 2000, will be as important in the liberal arts curriculum as history, political science, or a natural science is now. The college-wide courses in journalism will come into their own and give journalism teachers a wider influence as well as responsibility.

Some of the present controversies will have been settled by then. The merits of journalism education are scarcely debated bitterly any more although the skeptics survive. Journalism graduates will be the rule in all areas of mass communications which look to the schools for trained personnel, as in medicine and law today. Whether to get the bachelor's, master's, or doctor's degree will no longer puzzle students. The Ph.D. will be common, since in fifty years the substance of journalism for graduate study will have increased markedly.

The place of research, now unsettled, will have been decided by the creation of a relatively small number of schools that will make a specialty of such investigations and are equipped to do so with the computers and other machines that today are in the hands of a few wealthy industries or government agencies. These schools will serve as research centers; they will leave to the rest the general preparation for the vocation and the social science function.

Whether schools should concentrate on a few areas of communication or prepare their students for all areas likewise will have been determined. All but the research centers will prepare their students for every medium, not only because of the population pressures but also because of the drawing together, more and more, of the media themselves.

Basic preparation will be available in two ways: through fundamental

[117]

courses provided by the related schools and departments (such as chemistry, physics, engineering, and liberal arts) and through courses in principles of journalistic practice. The lines that now separate the media (magazines from newspapers, books from newspapers or magazines, and advertising from promotion, for example) no longer will exist. Schools of journalism will offer fewer but more elaborate courses. Editing, typography, printing, and photography will be one package. News reporting and writing will be taught, as it increasingly is now, from the standpoint of all media. So long as the media retain anything like their present physical characteristics, these operations, and others in the realms of advertising, circulation, and management, will be drawn together. In other words, the journalism education of the future will emphasize what the media do in common rather than their differences in procedure. Thus considerable integration in curriculum will take place.

Joint or conference teaching of subjects naturally will follow. Now to some extent practiced in basic courses in a few schools of journalism, it will be imperative fifty years from now because no teachers will possess the expertness to handle a course alone: mass communication will have become as complex as engineering, which is subdivided into numerous departments with relatively little interaction beyond an elementary stage.

Another area of debate—how broad shall be the geographical scope?—will have been settled, for transportation and communication will have been so speeded that no student would be properly prepared for the occupation if he knew American journalism only. In the past decade, journalism education has become considerably more international. If an atomic war is avoided the result may be a much more closely related body of nations in which citizens of any one might expect to work in another, and would therefore need to know more about the journalism of other nations.

Methods of instruction in journalism will be different in several ways: There will be closer relationship to the profession. Consequently there will be less tendency to evaluate and criticize the media because of this relationship, for courses will be heavily technical and practical, of necessity. This protects an occupation from social criticism (as witness science until the development of the atomic bomb). Except in journalism courses that are closer to the social studies than to the physical sciences (history, principles, and ethics, for instance) textbooks will have little place, for much of the instruction will be by practical laboratory work, use of many varieties of audio-visual aids, and internships in the field.

Journalism education, then, is destined to become at one and the same time (1) more technical in its orientation, because journalism will have become more technically complex; and (2) a greater force for intelligent use and understanding of the media of mass communication. Such education will be assumed. It will be offered by all institutions of higher education. More departments and schools than ever before will be in operation. Within this group will be special institutes for research. Journalism will have assumed a place of civic importance that will force colleges and universities to provide all students with guidance for its use.

It will be a technical and descriptive education, however, rather than one heavily concerned with evaluation and criticism of the occupation. This characterization, insofar as it rests on an accurate forecast, is a danger against which present-day journalism educators must guard. Already denounced by some of their critics as mere handmaidens of the communications industry, journalism educators cannot afford to encourage a trend that will leave them powerless to perform one of the primary functions of education: to develop thinking people.

Bibliography

EVELYN SMITH

BOOKS

ANDERSON, T. W. "Probability Models for Analyzing Time Changes in Attitude," in Paul F. Lazarsfeld, *Mathematical Thinking in the Social Sciences.* Glencoe, Ill.: The Free Press, 1954.

ARGYLE, MICHAEL. *The Scientific Study of Social Behaviour.* New York: Philosophical Library, 1957.

ASH, PHILIP. *The Relative Effectiveness of Massed Versus Spaced Film Presentation* (Technical Report SDC 269-7-3). Port Washington, N. Y.: Department of the Navy, Special Devices Center, 1949.

BERELSON, BERNARD R., LAZARSFELD, PAUL F. AND MCPHEE, WILLIAM N. *Voting: A Study of Opinion Formation During a Presidential Campaign.* Chicago: The University of Chicago Press, 1954.

BIRD, GEORGE L. AND MERWIN, FREDERIC E. (eds). *The Press and Society.* New York: Prentice-Hall, 1951.

BLUMER, HERBERT. "The Public, the Crowd, and the Mass," in Alfred M. Lee Jr., *New Outline of the Principles of Sociology.* New York: Barnes and Noble, 1946.

BOGART, LEO. *The Age of Television.* New York: Frederick Ungar Publishing Co., 1956.

BRODBECK, EMIL E. *Handbook of Basic Motion Picture Techniques.* New York: Whittlesey House, 1950.

BUSH, CHILTON R. AND TEILHET, DARWIN. "The Press, Reader Habits, and Reader Interest," in American Academy of Political and Social Science, Philadelphia. *Press and the Contemporary Scene.* Philadelphia: 1942. (Its Annals, v. 219, January 1942).

CALLENBACH, ERNEST. *Our Modern Art, The Movies.* Chicago: Center for the Study of Liberal Education for Adults, 1955.

CHERRY, COLIN. *On Human Communication, a Review, a Survey and a Criticism.* New York: Wiley, 1957.

COOPER, KENT. *Barriers Down.* New York: Farrar and Rinehart, 1942.

[121]

EDWARDS, ALLEN L. *Techniques of Attitude Scale Construction.* New York: Appleton-Century-Crofts, 1957.

EMERY, EDWIN, AND SMITH, HENRY LADD. *The Press and America.* New York: Prentice-Hall, 1954.

FELDMAN, JOSEPH AND FELDMAN, HARRY. *Dynamics of the Film.* New York: Hermitage House, 1952.

FESTINGER, LEON. "Informal Social Communication," in Dorwin Cartwright and Alvin Zander, *Group Dynamics: Research and Theory.* Evanston, Ill.: Row, Peterson, 1953.

FESTINGER, LEON, SCHACHTER, STANLEY AND BUCK, KURT. *Social Pressures in Informal Groups.* New York: Harper, 1950.

FLESCH, RUDOLF. *How to Test Readability.* New York: Harper, 1951.

FREIDSON, ELIOT. "Communications Research and the Concept of the Mass," in Wilbur Schramm, *The Process and Effects of Mass Communication.* Urbana: University of Illinois Press, 1954.

GERNSHEIM, HELMUT. *The History of Photography.* London: Oxford University Press, 1955.

GRAMLING, OLIVER. *AP—The Story of the News.* New York: Farrar and Rinehart, 1940.

GRIFFITH, RICHARD. *The World of Robert Flaherty.* New York: Duell, Sloane and Pearce, 1953.

GUTTMAN, LOUIS. "A New Approach to Factor Analysis: the Radex," in Paul F. Lazarsfeld, *Mathematical Thinking in the Social Sciences.* Glencoe, Ill.: The Free Press, 1954.

HARDY, FORSYTH. *Grierson on the Documentary.* London: Collins, 1946.

HERZOG, HERTA. "What Do We Really Know About Daytime Serial Listeners," in Paul F. Lazarsfeld and Frank N. Stanton, *Radio Research 1942-3.* New York: Duell, Sloane and Pearce, 1944.

HOBAN, CHARLES F., JR. *Some Aspects of Learning from Films.* State College, Pa.: The Pennsylvania State College, Instructional Film Research Program, 1949.

HOMANS, GEORGE C. *The Human Group.* New York: Harcourt, 1950.

HORAN, JAMES D. *Mathew Brady, Historian With a Camera.* New York: Crown Publishers, 1955.

HOVLAND, CARL I. "Effects of the Mass Media of Communication," in Gardner Lindzey, *Handbook of Social Psychology.* Cambridge, Mass.: Addison-Wesley Publishing Co., 1954.

HOVLAND, CARL I., JANIS, IRVING L. AND KELLEY, HAROLD H. *Communication and Persuasion.* New Haven: Yale University Press, 1953.

Bibliography

HOVLAND, CARL I., LUMSDAINE, ARTHUR A. AND SHEFFIELD, FRED D. *Experiments in Mass Communications* (Studies in Social Psychology in World War II, Vol. III). Princeton, N. J.: Princeton University Press, 1949.

HOVLAND, CARL I. and others. *The Order of Presentation in Persuasion.* New Haven: Yale University Press, 1957.

HUGHES, HELEN MACGILL. *News and the Human Interest Story.* Chicago: University of Chicago Press, 1940.

HYMAN, HERBERT. *Survey Design and Analysis.* Glencoe, Ill.: The Free Press, 1955.

JACKSON, ROBERT. *Learning from Kinescopes and Films* (Technical Report SDC-20-TV-1). Port Washington, N. Y.: Department of the Navy, Special Devices Center, 1952.

JACOBS, LEWIS. *The Rise of the American Film.* New York: Harcourt, Brace, 1939.

KATZ, ELIHU AND LAZARSFELD, PAUL F. *Personal Influence: The Part Played by People In the Flow of Mass Communcations.* Glencoe, Ill.: The Free Press, 1955.

KLAPPER, JOSEPH T. "The Comparative Effects of the Various Media," in Wilbur Schramm, *The Process and Effects of Mass Communication.* Urbana: University of Illinois Press, 1954.

KLAPPER, JOSEPH T. *The Effects of Mass Media.* New York: Bureau of Applied Social Research Columbia University, 1949.

KLAPPER, JOSEPH T. "Mass Media and Persuasion," in Wilbur Schramm, *The Process and Effects of Mass Communication.* Urbana: University of Illinois Press, 1954.

KLARE, GEORGE R. AND BUCK, BYRON. *Know Your Reader.* New York: Hermitage House, 1954.

LASSWELL, HAROLD D. "The Structure and Function of Communication in Society," in Wilbur Schramm, *Mass Communications.* Urbana: University of Illinois Press, 1949.

LASSWELL, HAROLD D., LEITES, NATHAN, and associates. *Language of Politics: Studies in Quantitative Semantics.* Buffalo, N. Y.: Stewart, 1949.

LAZARSFELD, PAUL F. *Radio and the Printed Page.* New York: Duell, Sloan and Pearce, 1940.

LAZARSFELD, PAUL F. (ed.). *Mathematical Thinking in the Social Sciences.* Glencoe, Ill.: The Free Press, 1954.

LAZARSFELD, PAUL F., BERELSON, BERNARD AND GAUDET, HAZEL. *The People's Choice.* New York: Columbia University Press, 1948.

LAZARSFELD, PAUL F. AND ROSENBERG, MORRIS (eds.). *The Language of Social Research*. Glencoe, Ill.: The Free Press, 1955.

LAZARSFELD, PAUL F. AND STANTON, FRANK N. *Communications Research 1948-49*. New York: Harper, 1949.

LAZARSFELD, PAUL F. AND STANTON, FRANK N. *Radio Research 1941*. New York: Duell, Sloan and Pearce, 1941.

LAZARSFELD, PAUL F. AND STANTON, FRANK N. *Radio Research 1942-43*. New York: Duell, Sloan and Pearce, 1944.

LIKERT, RENSIS AND HAYES, SAMUEL P., JR. (eds.). *Some Application of Behavioural Research*. Paris: UNESCO, 1957.

MCPHEE, WILLIAM N. *New Strategies for Research in the Mass Media*. New York: Bureau of Applied Social Research, Columbia University, 1946.

MCCLUSKY, FREDERICK DEAN. *The Audio-Visual Bibliography*. Dubuque: Wm. C. Brown, 1955.

MCTAVISH, C. L. *Effect of Repetitive Film Showings on Learning* (Technical Report SDC 269-7-12). Port Washington, N. Y.; Department of the Navy, Special Devices Center, 1949.

MANVELL, ROGER. *Film*. Baltimore: Penguin Books, 1946.

MANVELL, ROGER. *The Film and the Public*. Baltimore: Penguin Books, 1955.

MERTON, ROBERT K. *Mass Persuasion*. New York: Harper, 1946.

MERTON, ROBERT K. "Patterns of Influence: A Study of Interpersonal Influence and Communications Behavior in a Local Community," in Paul F. Lazarsfeld and Frank N. Stanton, *Communications Research, 1948-49*. New York: Harper, 1949.

MERTON, ROBERT K. *Social Theory and Social Structure*. Glencoe, Ill.: The Free Press, 1957.

MILLER, JOE ALEX. *Deadline Every Minute*. Garden City, N. Y.: Doubleday, 1957.

MOTT, FRANK LUTHER. *The News in America*. Cambridge: Harvard University Press, 1952.

NELSON, H. E., MOLL, K. R. AND JASPEN, N. *Comparison of the Audio and Video Elements of Instructional Films*. (Technical Report SDC 269-7-18). Port Washington, N. Y.: Department of the Navy, Special Devices Center, 1950.

NEWCOMB, THEODORE M. "An Approach to the Study of Communicative Acts," in A. Paul Hare, et al., *Small Groups: Studies in Social Interaction*. New York: Knopf, 1955.

NEWHALL, BEAUMONT. *The History of Photography.* New York: The Museum of Modern Art, 1949.

News Agencies, Their Structure and Operation. Paris: UNESCO, 1953.

NICHOLS, M. E. *(CP)—The Story of the Canadian Press.* Toronto: The Ryerson Press, 1948.

1958 International Year Book. New York: Editor & Publisher, 1958.

OSGOOD, CHARLES E. and others. *The Measurement of Meaning.* Urbana,: University of Illinois Press, 1957.

PARSONS, TALCOTT. *The Social System.* Glencoe, Ill.: The Free Press, 1951.

PARSONS, TALCOTT AND SHILS, EDWARD A. (eds.). *Toward a General Theory of Action.* Cambridge: Harvard University Press, 1951.

PHILLIPS, CABELL, (ed.). *Dateline: Washington.* Garden City, N. Y.: Doubleday, 1949.

ROSE, ARNOLD M. "Three Types of Human Association: The Crowd, the Audience, and the Public," in his *Sociology: The Study of Human Relations.* New York: Knopf, 1956.

ROSENBERG, BERNARD AND WHITE, DAVID MANNING. *Mass Culture: The Popular Art in America.* Glencoe, Ill.: The Free Press, 1957.

ROTHA, PAUL. *Documentary Film.* New York: Funk & Wagnalls, 1952.

ROTHA, PAUL, AND GRIFFITH, RICHARD. *The Film Till Now.* New York: Funk & Wagnalls, 1949.

ROTHSTEIN, ARTHUR. *Photojournalism.* New York: American Photographic Book Publishing Co., 1956.

SCHACHTER, STANLEY. "Deviation, Rejection, and Communication," in Dorwin Cartwright and Alvin Zunder, *Group Dynamics: Research and Theory.* Evanston, Ill.: Row, Peterson, 1953.

SCHRAMM, WILBUR. *Responsibility in Mass Communication.* New York: Harper, 1957.

SIMON, HERBERT A. *Models of Man: Social and Rational.* New York: Wiley, 1957.

SIMON, HERBERT A. "Some Strategic Considerations in the Construction of Social Science Models," in Paul F. Lazarsfeld, *Mathematical Thinking in the Social Sciences.* Glencoe, Ill.: The Free Press, 1954.

STARR, CECILE. *Ideas on Film.* New York: Funk & Wagnalls, 1951.

SPOTTISWOODE, RAYMOND. *Film and its Techniques.* Berkeley: University of California Press, 1952.

SPOTTISWOODE, RAYMOND. *A Grammar of the Film.* Berkeley: University of California Press, 1950.

STOREY, GRAHAM. *Reuters*. New York: Crown Publishers, 1951.

VANDERMEER, ABRAM W. *Relative Effectiveness of Instruction by: Films Exclusively, Films Plus Study Guides, and Standard Lecture Methods* (Technical Report SDC-269-7-13). Port Washington, N. Y.: Department of the Navy, Special Devices Center, 1950.

WIEBE, GERHART D. "Mass Communications," in Eugene L. Hartley and Ruth E. Hartley, *Fundamentals of Social Psychology*. New York: Knopf, 1952.

WILLIAMS, FRANCIS. *Transmitting World News*. Paris: UNESCO, 1953.

WIRTH, LOUIS. "Consensus and Mass Communication," in Wilbur Schramm, *Mass Communications*. Urbana: University of Illinois Press, 1949.

World Communications: Press, Radio, Film, Television. Paris: UNESCO, 1956.

ARTICLES AND PAMPHLETS

BREED, WARREN. "Newspaper 'Opinion Leaders' and the Process of Standardization," *Journalism Quarterly*, XXXII (Summer, 1955), 227-84, 328.

BRONOKOWSKI, J. "Planning for the Year 2000," *The Nation*, CLXXXVI (March 22, 1958), 248-50.

BUSH, CHILTON R. "Notes on a New Method for Determining 'Newspaper Audience,'" *Journalism Quarterly*, XIX (December, 1942), 371-74.

"Business Paper Advertising Trend Is to Few Books, Big Space, Color," *Industrial Marketing*, XLIII (January, 1958), 44-5.

BUZBY, G. CARROLL. "I Predict: A Growing Industrial Press," *Printers' Ink*, CCLXI (December 27, 1957), 54.

CASEY, RALPH D. "The Challenge to Journalism Education," *Journalism Quarterly*, XXXII (Winter, 1955), 39-45.

"Communications Aided by Times Facsimile," *Editor & Publisher*, XCI (February 22, 1958), 44.

CORT, DAVID. "The Scandalous Ad-Tax," *The Nation*, CLXXXVI (January 18, 1958), 52-3.

CUTLIP, SCOTT M. "Content and Flow of AP News—from Trunk to TTS to Reader," *Journalism Quarterly*, XXXI (Fall, 1954), 434-46.

DUGAN, GEORGE, "Dead Sea Scrolls Swiftly Indexed by Electric Computer," *The New York Times*, CVII (March 28, 1958), 27.

DURNIAK, JOHN. "Will Tape Replace Film?" *Popular Photography,* XXLV (February, 1958), 76-79, 102-6.

GALLUP, GEORGE. "Changes in the Newspaper During the Next 20 Years," *Journalism Quarterly,* XXXII (Winter, 1955), 17-20, 38.

GIEBER, WALTER. "Across the Desk: A Study of 16 Telegraph Editors," *Journalism Quarterly,* XXXIII (Fall, 1956), 423-32.

GOULD, JACK. "Wonder of Type," *The New York Times,* CVII (May 4, 1958), X 11.

HIBBS, BEN. *Magazines—Past Present Future, An Address Delivered at the Meeting of the Public Relations Society of America, at Philadelphia, Pa., November 18, 1957.* Philadelphia: *The Saturday Evening Post,* n.d.

HYMAN, HERBERT H. "Toward a Theory of Public Opinion," *Public Opinion Quarterly,* XXI (Spring, 1957), 56.

JANIS, I. L. "Personality Correlates of Susceptibility to Persuasion," *Journal of Personality,* XXII (1954), 504-18.

JONES, ROBERT L. "A Psychometric Study of Minnesota Industrial Editors," *Journalism Quarterly,* XXXIV (Spring, 1957), 253-55.

KATZ, ELIHU. "The Two-Step Flow of Communication: An Up-To-Date Report on a Hypothesis," *Public Opinion Quarterly,* XXI (Spring, 1957), 61.

KAY, HERBERT. "Toward an Understanding of News Reading Behavior," *Journalism Quarterly,* XXXI (Winter, 1954), 15-32, 94.

KLAPPER, JOSEPH T. "Mass Media and the Engineering of Consent," *The American Scholar,* XVII (Autumn, 1948), 419-29.

KLAPPER, JOSEPH T. "What We Know About the Effects of Mass Communication: The Brink of Hope," *Public Opinion Quarterly,* XXI (Winter 1957-58), 453-74.

LARSEN, ROY E. "I Predict: Magazines Will Become More Important," *Printers' Ink,* CCLXI (December 27, 1957), 55-56.

LARUE, ARLENE C. "What Will Women Be Like in 1980?" *Syracuse Herald-Journal,* LXXXII (April 4, 1958), 13.

LAZARSFELD, PAUL F. "Public Opinion and the Classical Tradition," *Public Opinion Quarterly,* XXI (Spring, 1957), 39-54.

MACCOBY, ELEANOR E. "Why Do Children Watch Television?", *Public Opinion Quarterly,* XVIII (Fall, 1954), 239-44.

MCGINNIS, A. R. *How Can International Advertising Influence the Future of Business Publications: An Address Delivered at the Chicago Regional Conference of the National Business Publications, Inc.,*

[127]

at Chicago, Ill., October 7, 1957. Washington: National Business Publications, 1957.

"Magazine Articles Abstracted Electronically," *A News Release Issued by the Institute of Radio Engineers, Inc.,* New York, March 24, 1958.

"Media Forecast," *Tide,* XXXII (January 10, 1958), 43.

MERZEL, HERBERT AND KATZ, ELIHU. "Social Relations and Innovation in the Medical Profession," *Public Opinion Quarterly,* IX (Winter, 1955-56), 337-52.

MOSKOWITZ, MILTON. "Ziff-Davis Sees Rosy Future for Specialized Magazine Titles," *Advertising Age,* XXVI (August 8, 1955), 82.

MOTT, FRANK LUTHER. "Magazines and Books, 1975: A Merging of Two Fields," *Journalism Quarterly,* XXXII (Winter, 1955), 21-6.

NIXON, RAYMOND B. "Changes in Readers Attitude Toward Daily Newspapers," *Journalism Quarterly,* XXXI (Fall, 1954), 421-33.

NIXON, RAYMOND B. "Who Will Own the Press in 1975?" *Journalism Quarterly,* XXXII (Winter, 1955), 10-16.

PETERSON, THEODORE, *Magazines of the 20th Century; An Address Delivered at the Annual Meeting of the American Agricultural Editors Association at Chicago, Illinois, December 4, 1957.* Urbana, Illinois: College of Journalism and Communications, University of Illinois, n.d.

"Printers' Ink Predicts for 1958," *Printers' Ink,* CCLXI (December 27, 1957), 34-42.

RAND, H. J. "Looking Ahead to 2000 A. D.," *Think,* XXIII (December, 1957), 7-9.

RAY, ROYAL H. "Advertising and Economic Support: 1955-1957," *Journalism Quarterly,* XXXII (Winter 1955), 31-38.

"Reinhold's Automatic Control Links Readership to Buying," *Mediascope,* II (February, 1958), 53.

SAWYER, SCOTTY. "Strictly Business—How Much Frequency?" *Tide,* XXXII (March 28, 1958), 46.

SCHRAMM, WILBUR. "Information Theory and Mass Communication," *Journalism Quarterly,* XXXII (Spring, 1955), 131-46.

SCHRAMM, WILBUR, "Measuring Another Dimension of Readership," *Journalism Quarterly,* XXIV (December 1947), 293-306.

SCHRAMM, WILBUR. "Twenty Years of Journalism Research," *Public Opinion Quarterly,* XXI (Spring, 1957), 91-107.

SCHRAMM, WILBUR AND WHITE, DAVID M. "Age, Education, Economic

Status: Factors in Newspaper Reading," *Journalism Quarterly,* XXVI (June, 1949), 149-59.

"Science Looks at Life in 2057 A. D.," *The New York Times Magazine,* CVII (December 8, 1957), 13, 100-01.

SIEBERT, FREDRICK S., "The Future of a Free Press," *Journalism Quarterly,* XXXII (Winter, 1955), 6-9.

"The Squeeze on Magazines," *Tide,* XXXI (December 13, 1957), 19-23.

SWANSON, CHARLES E. "What They Read in 130 Daily Newspapers," *Journalism Quarterly,* XXXII (Fall, 1955), 411-21.

TAYLOR, WILSON L. "Recent Developments in the Use of 'Cloze Procedure,' " *Journalism Quarterly,* XXXIII (Winter, 1956), 42-48, 99.

TOLLEY, CAROL BICK. "Media Outlook," *Tide,* XXXII (March 28, 1958), 56.

"Why Have We Changed Our Editorial Style?" *Advertising Agency,* LI (January 3, 1958), 9.

WIEBE, GERHART D. "A New Dimension in Journalism," *Journalism Quarterly,* XXXI (Fall, 1954), 411-20.

WIEBE, GERHART D. "Radio and Television: Looking Ahead 20 Years," *Journalism Quarterly,* XXXII (Winter, 1955), 27-30.

"The Year 2000: Automobile on Air?", *Newsweek,* LI (April 7, 1958), 79.

Topical Index

Journalism education (*see also* Mass communications research)
case method of instruction, vi
conflicting views, v-vi
early history, v
and liberal education, vii
new areas, vi
predictions on future development, 116-119

Magazines
advertising, 53, 57-58
automation predictions, 50-51, 60
changes in content, 51, 58
circulation, 53-54, 58
editorial content, 54, 58
general circulation type, 1
international distribution, 58
management problems and practices, 54-56, 59
number published, 53
political, 59
production, 56-57, 60
promotion, 55-56, 60
propagandistic, 59
research, 57, 60
types published, 53, 59

Mass communications
principal instruments, 1
relation to journalism, vii

Mass communications research
aims, 95
changing character, 100-101
concepts of mass media and mass communications, 103-107
definition difficulties, 103-107
"functional" research approach, 96
journalism education, objectives, 98-99
journalism research, expansion, 99-100
journalism research, relationships, 97-103

new concepts of impersonal and interpersonal communications, 107-111
problems of measuring effect, 109-110
relationship to other research areas, 111-113
research areas, current and future, 113
research implications of lack of definition, 105-107
research perspective changes, 99
two-step flow theory, 107-109

Newspapers; *see* Daily newspapers; Weekly newspapers

Periodicals; *see* Magazines

Photography; *see* Photojournalism

Photojournalism
artistic responsibility, 90-91
automation effects, 89-90
creativity, 91-92
early history, 87-88
in outer space, 90
predictions of new processes, 89-90

Population growth
cause of injustice, 11
resulting problems for newspapers, 7-9

Public interest
definition, 4
growth, 4

Publicity as law enforcement, 13-14

Public relations as communications experts, 10